DNA of Dalit Movement

DNA of Dalit Movement

Ojha Jai Prakash

PARTRIDGE
A Penguin Random House Company

ISBN:	Hardcover	978-1-4828-1884-0
	Softcover	978-1-4828-1883-3
	Ebook	978-1-4828-1882-6

To order additional copies of this book, contact
Partridge India
000 800 10062 62
www.partridgepublishing.com/india
orders.india@partridgepublishing.com

Essays

The book is a collection of essays written by the author on issues that are related to the dalits. The author has touched upon topics that are at the vortex of highly engrossing debates, currently in vogue in India. The presentation style is lucid and simple so as to enable even an ordinary reader to grasp the nitty gritty of dalit polity and the impact it is creating on the socio political terrain of contemporary India.

Preface

Enough has been written about who constitute dalits and how they had been treated, ever since the institution of caste came into being, under an oppressive brahminical social structure where the caste hierarchy was very rigid and stratified. Dalit is not a caste unto itself but rather refers to the multitude of lower castes and communities that have been historically deprived both in terms of material benefits and dignity. Dalits resisted, organized themselves and took to the streets asking for better treatment. They were led in their efforts by some of the greatest social reformers of our time like Jyoti Phule, Ambedkar and Periyar. Even the Congress party, the only major party in pre independence years, was compelled to take the dalit aspirations into account, with leaders like Mahatma Gandhi realizing the need to bring the dalits into the freedom struggle movement and founding Harijan Sabha to do welfare works for the lower castes. Ambedkar's differences with the then Congress leadership, particularly, with Gandhi on issues related to dalits have also been incorporated in this book. Though eyebrows have been raised on the role of Ambedkar in the national freedom movement, the fact that he was a true humanist and nationalist can't be denied. He worked towards removing the internal contradictions of the society to make it more equal and egalitarian. In course of time, dalit leadership grew and soon they were joined by dalit bureaucrats, academicians, activists and a section of the dalit social elites which took the shape of a movement. The book gives a brief account of the trajectory of the growth of the dalit movement starting from the demand for restoration of civil rights to the lower castes to the removal of caste based discriminations against them and then ultimately, to the demand for more representation in legislatures and bureaucracy. Today, though the dalit movement has emerged as a powerful pressure lobby which cannot be taken lightly by the ruling classes, it has not got the critical mass in our joint electorate system to alter the course of Indian polity on its own terms and conditions. However, despite the limitations the movement is perhaps one of the most remarkable subaltern upsurges that resulted in incorporation of various provisions for the empowerment and welfare of the dalits in the constitution without any real opposition from any quarter.

The book contemplates to analyze the reasons behind the failure of the dalit upsurge to transform into a potent force to challenge the forces of status quo or take up issues that affect the lives of maximum number of the dalits in the country. The dalit agenda seems to be hijacked by the urban elites among them who seem to be more bothered about reservation and issues like Ambedkar cartoons or statements of Asish Nandy that may be emotional but devoid of any mala fide intention. Most of the dalit population lives in rural areas of the country where the structure of economy is such that land is intrinsically linked to social status and prestige. Majority dalit population is either landless or marginal peasant; the so called land reforms have failed to reach them and yet the mainstream dalit leadership remains blissfully ignorant of this. The neo liberal globalization phase has posed a grave threat to the very concept of reservation/social justice, the subsidies to the vulnerable sections of our population are being pruned in the name of fiscal discipline, the social assistance welfare programmes of the state are being curtailed and government is being downsized but unfortunately, the dalit leadership/intelligentsia has not managed to develop an economic vision that tends to mitigate the sufferings of the neo reforms. Apart from demands for reservation in the private sector and vague talks of dalits becoming capitalists leading to dalit capitalism, the movement has not articulated the major concerns of the dalit masses that have been left behind from the spread over or trickle down benefits of liberalization. The new reforms have hardly resulted in betterment in the living conditions of majority of the lower castes and instead, have led to widening socio economic inequalities between the better off and poorer sections of our population.

The dalit polity has also been challenged by the forces of Mandalisation and Hindutva. After the implementation of the Mandal Commission Report, the empowerment process of the backwards led to increase in their political clout and many OBC leaders gained visibility. The Hindi heartland saw the emergence of OBC leadership at the helm of affairs in key states like Bihar and UP. Since the backward leadership was also part of the social justice plank as the dalits, it was expected that the political coalition between both would result in the marginalization of the upper castes in the political landscape of the country. The outcome was not on expected lines. Ground level hostilities owing to conflict of interests between the backwards and dalits on the farmlands led to political rivalry between the two. The most populous Indian state of Uttar Pradesh is home to direct electoral contests between the Samajwadi Party and the Bahujan Samaj Party, with both of them widely seen to be representing the OBCs and the dalits respectively. The most glaring aspect of politics in the state is the prevalence of animosity between the dalits and the OBCs and from time to time, the simmering tensions between the two camps lead to outbreak of violence on the streets. Things have taken such a turn that today, the dalit leadership is not averse to joining hands with the Hindutva forces to keep the backwards out of the power equation as witnessed in the state on certain occasions. The Dravidian movement has till now only paid lip service to the dalit cause and probably, is more non Brahmin than anti Brahmin. The social revolution which heralded the birth of the Dravidian parties in Tamil Nadu and led to the political decline of the Congress by challenging its predominantly upper caste leadership has benefitted the backwards more. The anti caste message has not reached the masses and there is no major dalit party in Tamil Nadu which is in a position to challenge the mainstream Dravidian parties. Reports of caste conflicts between the dalits and the major peasant castes in the state keep surfacing from time to time.

The Hindutva forces talk about cultural nationalism implying the philosophy of one nation, one religion, one language and one culture. This is anathema to the dalit movement that talks of an exclusive identity and cultural distinctiveness from the Hindus and this is reflected in the alacrity with which a section of the dalit leadership/intelligentsia has embraced Buddhism which was supposed to provide a platform for the dalits to escape from the tyranny of Hinduism. The dalit leadership is apprehensive that too close identification with the right wing groups will culminate in the loss of dalit social agenda and ultimately, will pose a threat to their identity that may face the danger of being submerged under the broader Hindu identity. The arrival of the right wing forces in a grand way in Indian polity post 1990 is not a mere coincidence. Mandalisation process created fissures in Hindu society with the growing assertions of the OBCs and the Hindutva plank of a unified Hindu society appeared to be in tatters. To counter this Mandal challenge, the right wing forces sought to cultivate a consolidated Hindu identity by raising issues like building of Ram temple at Ayodhya, Hindu nationalism, uniform civil code etc. and attacking the Congress/other parties of minority appeasement and pseudo secularism. The dalit strategy of projecting themselves as victims of exploitative Hindu social order to gain concessions from the state, based on caste, is not likely to find favours with the Hindutva forces that place premium on unity of different social groups within the ambit of Hinduism. However despite the apprehensions, the dalit leadership joined hands with the Hindutva BJP to form government thrice in Uttar Pradesh. Bhimshakti and Shivshakti alliance in Maharashtra has been forged in the past. Despite all the hue and cry of a separate religion for the dalits in the form of Buddhism and the conversion of dalits from Hinduism to Buddhism on the exhortation of dalit leaders, the fact remains that even today; more than 90 percent of the dalits are practising Hindus. In Maharashtra, most of the members of the Mahar community have converted to Buddhism but they have not been able to make a strong statement politically while in UP, most of the dalits did not bite the Buddhism bait and yet, they are the most empowered among the dalits on a national scale. The conversion phenomenon did not yield anything concrete to the dalit movement and apart from providing solace in the form of a separate paradigm, it failed to galvanize them to the desired extent.

Relations between the dalit leadership and the communists have also been analyzed. Though their engagement should have been natural considering the fact that both of them have the same support bases of agricultural labourers and working people, the inter relationship was marked by mutual suspicion and distrust. The dalits were annoyed at the proclivity of the communists to see all the problems in terms of class, rather than caste. For the dalit leadership, all the problems in Indian context have their genesis in caste. Even within the supposedly secular unions, separate SC/ST cells are there. Urbanization and capitalism have led to more and more democratization of public spaces, caste markers associated with occupational structures are slowly but steadily decreasing in influence as jobs are getting automated, the middle classes have made their presence felt in our polity; what does all these developments point to? Caste as a factor in Indian polity can't be denied today but whether it will stride on the streets of political India as a colossus in the future remains to be seen. The electorate is getting more enlightened, the level of education and empowerment is going upwards and issues like governance and corruption can no longer be warped under the carpet.

Dalits have suffered immensely for centuries because of their caste which prevented their social intercourse with the rest of the population. Ambedkar called for the annihilation of castes. Caste creates hierarchy which makes the social integration process difficult, creating abyss between different castes and communities. However, despite this, the dalit leadership or the intelligentsia wants the institution of caste to survive because this provides them ample opportunities to play the victim card and get concessions from the state. Caste has become a resource for political mobilization and canvassing.

The book also talks about the dilemma facing the dalit groups in the joint electorate system, once their demand for separate electorates did not find resonance with the top national leadership of the time. The needs of parliamentary democracy—multi party system, discipline with party ranks, issue of party whips and the hold of the top leadership on the party apparatus—all these ensured that the dalit leaders of various parties had to toe the party line on policies that were not necessarily pro dalit. The dalit parties that sprung up in Maharashtra, Tamil Nadu or UP tended to acquire sectarian overtures and became enmeshed in politics of exclusion. They could not forge a unity of purpose with the other parties even on matters that reflected secular concerns.

The politics behind reservation also finds mention in the book which has led to the fragmentation of the once considered monolithic dalit unity and solidarity, with various marginalized social groups within the dalit community, joining the chorous of demand for separate reservation for them. Apart from reservation, the dalit leadership has failed to throw up a viable alternative for empowerment, especially at the time when there has been a sharp decline in opportunities for public employment. Reservation, as a concept, has outlived its utility. Though it has been in vogue for more than sixty years, majority of the dalit population still lacks reasonable human development indices. The benefits of reservation has only gone to a minority lower caste population who has climbed up the socio economic ladder and are refusing to look downwards. They have forgotten their fellow brethren and are not interested in letting reservation be extended towards them. Politics associated with social justice and reservation has assumed centrifugal dimensions with several communities jostling with each other in support of their demands even if these acts threaten social cohesion. The politicians, rather than thinking about the nation as a whole, tend to develop a fractured line and identify themselves more with their vote banks. The clamour for reservation has gone up to such an extent that even the constitutionally prescribed ceiling of 50 percent reservation looks to be inadequate in pandering to the competitive reservation demands of various communities.

The Indian political terrain is home to various kinds of contestations from different subaltern groups who want to leave an imprint on our democracy. They were previously denied spaces in our democracy and their voices carried no weight. The deepening democratization process gave them electoral clout and the courage to depict their own alternate view points, ideology and convictions at public spaces in the form of idols and monuments. This insulted the traditional political power centres who felt that it was only their prerogative to construct national symbols. The politics of symbolism denoted by a construction spree of statues of dalit icons and Ambedkar parks may have led to a sense of pride and dignity among the dalit masses in UP but it has not resulted in betterment in their quality of life. The non dalits are not too much impressed with the construction of the idols of the dalit icons and this has culminated in protests against the construction drive. The political empowerment/mobilization may have begun but the social transformation in rural UP is yet to be deciphered.

Dalit Movement: An introduction to its growth trajectory in Indian Context

Ever since the birth of the human civilization, India, in the true sense, has never been a nation. When we examine the demographic profile of the nation right from the days of the Aryan period, the first thing that strikes us, is the fact that the population was never homogeneous. Hordes of invaders like the Huns, Kushans, Arabs and Greeks etc. kept pouring into the country through north western Himalayan passes. Many of them settled here owing to fertile soil and a better climate. Inter racial mingling was no taboo. The political boundaries were not defined and India was divided into numerous kingdoms which were all involved into a perpetual struggle among them to extend their areas of influence. The region, south of the Vindhayas, was relatively peaceful as the invaders from the north west were hardly in a position to penetrate deeper south into the Indian peninsula due to difficult terrain. Except for periods during the reign of Mauryan and Mogul rulers, the political unity of the entire nation could not be achieved. Achieving a political unification was an arduous task as there were a plethora of races like the Mongoloids, the Aryans, the Dravidians, the Mediterranean and of course, the indigenous tribal population of central India who were of the Proto Australoid stock. The linguistic profile was also varied. The people of the north spoke in Aryan languages while people way down into the south had their own scripts and languages. During the Sultanate and the Mogul periods, Persian got the impetus. The tribals and the other marginalized communities spoke in their own dialects/languages and practiced different customs. They were outside the pale of Aryan influence. Similar was the case with religions. Religions like Buddhism, Jainism and Sikhism have taken birth on Indian soil. There were believers as well as non believers.

After the arrival of the British in India, an efficient network of railways and roads, spread of modern education, commencement of posts and telegraphs and a unified command at the centre led to the development of a common perspective among the people from north to south and from east to west. The hatred against the common enemy (read British) brought about a sense of solidarity and oneness among the entire population of the country. Despite certain aberrations, the national freedom struggle succeeded in bringing the entire population on a common platform. It was the beginning of political unity and the nation. The Constitution was drafted to provide blue print to governance and achieve political consolidation of the country. To make our democracy more inclusive and durable, certain safeguards were provided to the marginalized communities to integrate them into the national mainstream. Though at the surface level, the task of managing the internal social contradictions appeared resolved, deep within the surface, fault lines remained.

Post independent India has witnessed momentous changes. Universal adult suffrage, periodic elections to the central and state legislatures and pulls & pressures of representative parliamentary democracy have given voices to those oppressed/marginalized communities that had remained at the periphery of our social mainstream. The social deepening of our democracy has brought to the fore the aspirations and dreams of the subaltern groups. The mandalisation of polity in the early nineties changed the face of Indian polity forever. The backward castes were numerically preponderant and constituted more than 40 percent of the population but despite this, the political leadership of the country had remained into the hands of the upper caste elites. Getting into the agitation mood, the backwards successfully challenged the socio political hegemony of the upper castes and as a testimony to this fact, the entire nation saw the catapultation of backward leadership at the helm of affairs in the northern Hindi heartland. Senior BJP leader Advani embarked on his famous Rath Yatra, pouring vitriol against the minority appeasement policy of the successive Congress governments, talking about Hindu pride and espousing for the cause of the construction of the Ram temple at Ayodhya in Uttar Pradesh. The entire nation became polarized on religious lines. Mandalisation of polity was sought to be fought by the Kamandalisation of polity. What is uniform in both the movements is the fact that both of them tended to place premium on identity politics. The mandalites were concerned about the backward sections of the population while the kamandalites wanted Hindu pride and if possible, Hindu Rashtra. None of them talked about a diverse inclusive India.

But long before the advent of these movements and even before the attainment of independence, the untouchables had organized themselves calling for an end to caste based discrimination. The book deals with the contours of the dalit movement, its brief history and whether it has succeeded in achieving its goals in contemporary India. The challenges confronting the movement and the internal contradictions have also been touched upon.

The dalit movement is regarded by many scholars as the most important social movement in India. While in the broader sense of the lower caste fights against the manuwadi hegemony, the dalit movement is as old as the institution of caste itself, the movement in the form of organized political resistance against oppression based on caste in the Hindu society, originated only during the colonial times. After the firm implantation of the colonial rule on the Indian soil, several changes started taking place. The social brahminical structures began to show signs of decay with the upper castes losing their supremacy in the new emerging societal dynamics. Indian Penal Code was introduced in 1861. Criminal Code Procedure got going in 1872. Both of these measures humanized our caste based justice delivery system. Spread of modern education and political thoughts based on rule of law and the creation of an equal egalitarian social set up provided a fertile ground for the breeding of various lower caste uprisings. Transformations induced during the colonial period, in the realm of social, political, economic and institutional environments gave a fillip to the aspirations of the depressed classes and facilitated the emergence of an organized resistance to the upper caste hegemony.

However, it needs to be emphasized that even before the arrival of the colonial masters; there have been movements like the Bhakti movement during the medieval times which laid stress on the universal brotherhood of mankind and monotheism. It asked the people to discard all sorts of superstitions, rituals and ceremonies and hence for this reason, it was a quintessential non Brahmin movement. People like Ramanujam, Ramananda, Kabir, Namdeo and Chaitanya were pioneers in creating a philosophical base for social equality. This movement gave a sense of pride and dignity to the lower caste people and encouraged their participation in public life. The preachers also contemplated to awaken the people to the dangers of caste discriminations. In the 19th century, the Arya Samaj, the Rama Krishna Mission and the Brahma Samaj advocated for the emancipation of untouchables and called for reforms within the Hindu religion by freeing it from the blemishes of superstition, caste and gender discriminations and excessive ritualism. Many scholars feel that the Hindu Renaissance movement was basically intended to neutralize the religious conversion drives of the Christian missionaries. Whatever the actual reasons may be, it can be said to the credit of these movements that they carried out an impartial analysis of the ills plaguing the Hindu society and tried their best to educate the masses of the evils of caste based discrimination system. They talked of co-optation of lower castes in the Hindu fold and giving them a dignified space in it. Many lower caste movements took place in the 19th and 20th centuries. The Satnamis movement in Madhya Pradesh, the Kuka movement of 1920 in Punjab, the Nadar Mahajana Sabha in Tamil Nadu and the Ezhava movement of Narayan Guru are some of the most remarkable uprisings in the surge towards the assertiveness of lower castes. These movements demonstrated that the lower castes were now no longer willing to take things lying down.

Jyoti Ba Phule is regarded as one of the most important figures in the field of social revolution. In 1873, he founded the Satya Shodak Samaj or the Society of Seekers of Truth to protect the members of lower caste communities from atrocities and exploitation. The Samaj opposed brahminical scriptures, idolatry and the Varna System and espoused the theory of rational thinking while rejecting the need for brahminical priestly class as educational and religious leaders. Phule's contribution also took note of the pulse of rural India when he advocated equal rights for peasants. He, along with his wife, opened schools/ colleges for education of women and the downtrodden class. His wonderful social movement lost its sheen when the members of the Samaj dissolved the body and merged it with the Congress. Chattrapati Sahu Maharaj of Kolhapur state was one of the earliest leaders who realized the importance of positive affirmative action plans for the lower castes. He subsidized education, opened several hostels in his state to facilitate education for lower castes and not only this, he also provided employment to them after completion of education.

One of the doyens of dalit movement was Periyar. The brutalities of the brahminical system changed him from a theist to an atheist. After joining Congress in 1919, he was elected as President of the Madras Presidency Congress Committee during the Tirupur session in 1922. His advocacy for reservation in government jobs and education for the depressed classes did not find resonance within the Congress and ultimately, he had to leave the party in 1925. Periyar is also credited with leading a non violent Satyagraha in Vaikom, Kerala for the fulfillment of temple entry programme of the depressed classes in 1924. His Self Respect Movement espoused social reforms, prevention of untouchability and caste based discrimination and exhorted the non Brahmins to have a sense of pride in their Dravidian past. In order to enlist the support of non Brahmins, the movement began to propagate an ideology of non Brahmin jati groups. Brahminical priesthood and Sanskritic social class values were blamed for the rampant inequalities in non Brahmin jati groups. In the wake of anti Hindi protests, Periyar was incarcerated. When the Justice Party weakened, its nomenclature was changed to Dravida Kazhagam. Imposition of Hindi and the ceremonies associated with brahminical priesthood were denounced. Periyar's vitriolic attacks on Tamil Brahmins and at times, recourse to physical violent attacks on them and denigration of Hindu gods and goddesses were acts that showed the militant side of the movement. It is no coincidence that the day of Indian independence on 15th August was celebrated as Black day by Periyar and his supporters.

All the movements directed at the emancipation of the depressed classes were generally localized in nature and there was nothing like a pan India dalit movement. The lower caste people were simmering with discontent and their leadership was annoyed with the Congress, the only major national party of the time, for repeatedly turning a blind eye to their plight. They also resented the upper caste influence on the Congress party and accused it of only furthering the cause of feudal forces and the Brahmins who would never shed their upper caste prejudices against the lower castes. It would not be an exaggeration to say that the pre Ambedkar reformers regarded the colonial rulers better than the Congress leadership and hence, at times they were not hesitant to support them, in lieu, of colonial favors like reservation in jobs and legislatures and enactment of socially progressive legislations to ameliorate their pitiful conditions. The movement could not get the desired impetus due to its limited spread and incongruence with the prevailing national mood of the time which was of resistance against the forces of colonialism and imperialism. The focus was also on the attainment of short term objectives like reservation and representation in government. Despite the obvious shortcomings, the movement did manage to achieve some tangible benefits to the depressed communities like access to public places and temples that were previously denied to them owing to their inferior social status. Moreover, the new found assertiveness of the lower castes forced the upper castes not to take the untouchables for granted. Even the upper caste leadership dominated Congress began to realize that the aspirations of downtrodden can no longer be swept under the carpet and the unfurling of social revolution is a national necessity to keep the nation united in its fight against the foreign domination.

However, the arrival of Dr. Ambedkar on the national stage in the 1920s set the ball rolling for the dalit movement in real terms. It is an undisputed fact that he was the most towering leader among the dalits. His vision and thoughts gave shape to the changing contours of dalit polity, starting from the mid 1920s to the mid 1950s and even today, more than 50 years after his death, the dalit polity has failed to find his suitable successor. Before presenting an anatomy of the movement, it will be interesting to take a glance at the various pro dalit initiatives of Ambedkar and his points of discord with the mainstream national leadership of that time, particularly with Mahatma Gandhi.

According to Ambedkar, the division of the Hindu society into castes and outcastes was the outcome of years and years of brahminical hegemony over the socio religious affairs of Hinduism. He commented that the Hindu civilization is a diabolical contrivance to suppress and enslave humanity. Its proper name would be infamy. He continued," What else can be said of a civilization which has produced a mass of people who are treated as an entity beyond human intercourse and whose mere touch is enough to cause pollution?" He founded the Bahiskrit Hitakarni Sabha to promote education and upliftment of the downtrodden communities. In the 1920s, he led a Satyagraha in Mahad to fight for the rights of the untouchables to draw water from the main tank of the town. The matter reached court and the court gave its verdict in favour of the untouchables. The popularity graph of Ambedkar soared as he began to undertake more agitations for the rights of the depressed classes to enter temples and gain access to public places. The dalit mobilization process took roots in the western parts of the country, especially in Maharashtra. Ambedkar castigated Hinduism for being unscientific and promoting superstitions. Not satisfied at this, he took the confrontation to another level by challenging the very notion of Varna and the caste hierarchy. He denounced the sacred religious texts of the Hindus and participated in the public burning of Manusmriti.

The views of Ambedkar and Congress were often at variance with each other on issues related to the dalit constituency with Ambedkar never missing an opportunity to lambast Congress for its upper caste mindset and anti dalit bias. On its part, Congress considered Ambedkar as a stumbling block in its overall endeavour of uniting the nation in the fight against the British forces. Whatever his critics may say—the fact of the matter was that, for Ambedkar, the dalit cause was supreme. For him, freedom from foreign rule was meaningless until and unless it was accompanied by a freedom for the dalit masses from the clutches of orthodox religious and social order. He was convinced that freedom was as repulsive as feudalism and once the freedom of the country was attained, the lower castes would face the same humiliation at the hands of the feudal Congress as they have been suffering from ages. Trained in western thoughts and notions of rationality, equality and rule of law, he seemed to acknowledge the imperial power as a lesser enemy than the upper caste dominated Congress. There were times when Ambedkar failed to understand the devious machinations of the British policy of divide and rule, much to the chagrin of the nationalist forces but despite this, his commitment for the cause of depressed classes cannot be underestimated. It is not fair to dub him anti nationalist, rather he should be complimented for consolidating the internal social groupings and later onwards, trying to amalgamate them with the rest of the population through his constitution. For him, internal contradictions of the Indian society had to be resolved first before embarking on the need for political freedom.

Ambedkar did not even spare Gandhi and took umbrage at the use of word Harijan for describing the dalit masses. He felt that the use of the term reflects an attitude that was too patronizing and condescending on the dalits. He did not take too kindly to Mahatma Gandhi's espousal of the Verna system. He considered Gandhi to be a typical Congressman whose love for dalits was a mere eye wash. Whatever may be the differences between the two stalwarts of our nation, it has to be accepted that both Ambedkar and Gandhi felt the need for improving the deplorable conditions of the untouchables. MK Gandhi saw the dalit problem from the perspective of an upper caste individual while Ambedkar saw it from the angle of depressed classes and all his bitterness towards caste prejudices stemmed from his personal experience of being born in the lower Mahar caste. Gandhi realized on his power of persuasion to bring in change in the attitudes of caste Hindus towards the untouchables by practising what he preached and taking up Harijan welfare work in their bastis. He tried to spread awareness about humane treatment of dalits and regarded caste discriminations as sinful and sub human behaviour. He founded Harijan Seva Sangh, a voluntary organization to work for dalit cause and travelled extensively throughout the country speaking against untouchability and the evils of caste system.

On the other hand, Ambedkar had an inherent distrust towards the attitudes of caste Hindus. He was of the firm conviction that caste Hindus are not going to reform themselves and they will always try to maintain the status quo, much to the detriment of the dalits. He advocated legal enactments to protect the interests of the depressed classes.

For any student of Indian polity, it is crystal clear that the original motive of MK Gandhi was to forge unity among different communities so that a common front can be presented in the fight against the British raj. Ambedkar's policy of exclusion, based on a separate identity for dalits, was proving to be an obstacle in the national freedom struggle. To counter Ambedkarism, Gandhi took to Harijan emancipation project to increase his acceptability among the dalits and wean them away from Ambedkar to the Congress fold. The Congress had very rightly realized that without the active participation of one fifth of masses, the national freedom struggle could not be sustained. Gandhi's heart beat for the depressed cannot be doubted as can be seen from the days of his initial struggle in South Africa when he fought for the civil rights of the blacks and the Asians in a racially segregated society. The confrontation between Gandhi and Ambedkar was a fall out of circumstances when both of them claimed to be the sole representative of the dalit constituency. Ambedkar thought that he represented the dalits while Gandhi felt he represented the whole of India, including dalits.

As a leading Indian scholar, Ambedkar was invited to testify before the Southborough Committee, busy in preparing the Government of India Act 1919. There, he argued for the creation of Separate Electorates and reservation for untouchables and other religious communities. He also participated in the 2nd Round Table Conference in 1932, held at London. Though Gandhi accepted separate electorates for various religious communities, he vociferously opposed separate electorates for the depressed communities on the ground that they were very much a part and parcel of Hindu society and Hindu unity should not be allowed to crumble. Gandhi began a fast unto death in the Yervada prison against the provisions of separate electorates. Apprehensive of communal reprisal and mass killings of dalits, Ambedkar agreed under massive coercion of the supporters of the Congress. Pune Pact was signed in 1932. This pact gave reservation to the dalits in the legislatures. According to dalit experts, Gandhi's fast was synonymous to blackmailing and the Pune pact denied a historic opportunity for the dalits to send their own representatives to the legislatures. This weakened the dalit movement as the joint electorate system diluted the intensity of sectarian dalit politics. **No doubt, the dalits had genuine reasons to feel aggrieved but at the same time, it cannot be denied that had the Mahatma not undertaken a fast on this issue and had Ambedkar succeeded in his design, there would have been unprecedented political mobilization of the dalits, leading to a possible balkanization of the country, on the lines of Jinnah's Pakistan.** Whatever may have been the arguments and counter arguments regarding the separate electorate issue, the fact remains that the Pune Pact prevented the possible rupturing of Indian polity on caste lines and facilitated the co-optation of dalits in the national fold with certain safeguards. The national freedom movement, already weakened by polarization on religious lines of Muslim League, would have suffered a further setback, had the separate electorate system been implemented. The Simon Commission (1930) had also rejected the separate electorate clause as it felt that, no doubt, it would have been the safest method of securing the return of adequate number of persons who enjoyed the confidence of the depressed classes, but it was averse to the very idea of stereotyping the differences between the depressed classes and the remainder of the Hindus by such a step which would introduce a new and a serious bar to their ultimate political amalgamation with the rest of the population.

Rather than feeling let down by the pact, the dalit leadership should take solace from the fact that dalit reservation once introduced in the legislature, later onwards became permanently ingrained in our polity, resulting in the extension of reservation from the legislatures to public employment to educational institutions. The dalits had not lost as it was a fair enough compromise between the caste Hindus and the dalits.

Ambedkar's sectarian politics, obsession with the dalit cause and refusal to come on the same platform as the Congress ensured his isolation from the national freedom movement. He also kept away from the communist vision of a casteless society as he felt that emphasis on class tends to dilute the ground realities in India. In 1936, he founded the Independent Labour party which won 15 seats in the 1937 elections to the Central Assembly. He set up the Scheduled Caste Federation of India but as bad luck would have it, his party fared badly in the elections, held in 1946, for the Constituent Assembly. Taking into account his unparalleled genius and intellectual capabilities, Congress supported him and he was elected to the Constituent Assembly where he played a stellar role as the President of the Constitution Drafting Committee. Later onwards, he joined Nehru's cabinet as union Labour minister from which he resigned over differences in the Hindu Code Bill with the more conservative elements within the party. During the last phase of his life, Ambedkar decided to renounce Hinduism and converted to Buddhism, with thousands of his followers, at Nagpur in 1956.

In the 1930s, Ambedkar came across as a fire brand dalit activist but in the later part of his life, he seemed to have mellowed down. He spent a considerable part of his political career in lampooning the Congress and even refused to accept Gandhi's claim to dalit leadership. Quite surprisingly, the same Ambedkar had no qualms in getting himself elected to the Constituent Assembly, riding on the back of Congress support. Not content at this, he went a step further and agreed to join the cabinet led by his bête noire Nehru. Now the question that puzzles the minds of most of the political observers is—Was it an act of political opportunism or was it, under compulsion or say, change in heart on the part of Ambedkar? It is very difficult to arrive at a definite conclusion but there were certain facts that one may find hard to conceal. Contrary to his claims of being the sole dalit spokesman, Ambedkar's appeal among the dalit masses was confined only in western part of the country, especially among the Mahar community to which he belonged. Gandhi and the Congress enjoyed a pan India appeal among the lower castes. It's another matter as of now; Ambedkarism was revisited after the mandalisation of polity and today, perhaps Ambedkar is the only leader whose statue can be seen in every nook and corner of the country and that too, without public funding. The Congress hold over the dalits has gradually decreased since the beginning of 1980s, a testimony to the increasing clout of the dalit parties like BSP.

Now getting back to the Congress-Ambedkar issue, there are certain questions that baffle many political observers even today. Despite being often at the receiving end of Ambedkar's ire, why did Congress get him elected to the Constituent Assembly and even made sure that he was elected as the President of the Constitution Drafting Committee? Some protagonists of the dalit movement feel that the co-optation of Ambedkar in the national scheme of things was not guided by any secular considerations or love for dalits but it was necessitated out of the need to buy Ambedkar's silence and keep the dalit flocks intact, preempting their move to drift in different directions. **The Congress knew that association of Ambedkar with the framing of our constitution would make sure that the dalits won't get antagonized by the constitutional provisions and accept them without any protest and at the same time, it was convinced that Ambedkar would not be able to impose his agenda on the Constituent Assembly, owing to its diverse composition.** They may be partially true but not fully. Though the Congress party comprised of the big landlords and the social composition was mostly upper caste who were not expected to champion the dalit cause, it cannot be denied that a considerable percentage of those people were avid social activists who worked with a missionary zeal for the poor and the downtrodden. Barring a few aberrations, most of the Congress leaders of that generation despite their feudal/

upper caste background firmly believed in secular and inclusive policy. They were products of the western liberal educational system and believed in the concept of nation built on strong foundations like rule of law, equality of rights and certain fundamental rights for all. Subtle forms of caste discriminations may have been prevalent even within the Congress but those were held under check by the towering personalities of Nehru and Gandhi. These may have been the reasons why they recognized the true potential of Ambedkar to contribute to the national and the dalit cause and made him the President of such an important body. The mutual acrimonious relation between the two was relegated to the background in the task of nation building.

The coming into force of the Indian Constitution on 26th January 1950 is a wonderful chapter in the annals of our history. The Indian constitution is the product of combined ethos, aspirations and outlook of our contemporary political leadership. The entire nation accepted the constitution in toto, without any grudge or misgivings towards the affirmative measures incorporated for the dalits. Of course, there were certain dissenting voices too but all of them were submerged for the making of our nascent democracy. This speaks volumes of the firm resolve/determination on the part of our political class which unlike our present leadership was not ready to buckle under the pressure/forces, inimical to national interests. The American blacks had to fight for years, even after the promulgation of the American constitution but here, in India, it was the farsightness of the founding fathers of our republic that the principle of one man—one vote and same value was accepted without any differences. It was the politics of inclusion that held sway. The concept of nation had arrived.

Many observers of Indian polity feel that the Indian constitution is a social contract between the dalits and the state. The welfare orientation of the state resulted in the implementation of positive affirmative action plans to improve the conditions of the dalits. It was widely acknowledged that dalits were not adequately represented in the realm of governance and administration. A conscious decision was made to reserve 15 percent seats for them in public employment. The reservation concept for the dalits was also extended to the legislatures to make sure that their voices are heard at the highest forums of parliamentary democracy. Seats have been reserved for the dalits in universities and other institutions of higher education. In the 1990s, reservation was made applicable for the dalits in the rural and urban local bodies to increase their clout at the grass root level democracy. A National Commission for scheduled castes and scheduled tribes was set up, under constitutional provision, to look after their grievances and suggest measures to offer them statutory protection from exploitation and atrocities. Later onwards, this body got bifurcated into National Commission for SCs and National Commission for STs. Article 17 abolished untouchability and its practice under any form was forbidden. Under its provision of the constitution, Untouchability Offences Act, 1955 was enacted and from 1976 onwards, this act was revamped as Civil Protection Act. An improved version of the Act which we are currently having is the SC & ST (Prevention of Atrocities) Act, 1989. All the above mentioned legislative enactments sought to protect the dalits from being subjected to caste based discriminations and humiliation. The Employment of Manual Scavengers and Construction of Dry Latrines (prohibition) Act, 1993 was a step taken in the right direction to protect the dignity of dalits as human beings. However, even today, it is common to find that most of the people engaged in such jobs, belong to Bhangi communities.

Apart from the dalit specific issues, there are certain features of our constitution like the Directive Principles of State Policy in Chapter 1V that enjoins upon the state to take up issues like social equity, social justice and equitable distribution of resources, social assistance programmes for old age, unemployment, sickness & disablement, maternity relief, equal pay for men and women etc. These measures, though not directly related to dalits, help them, considering the fact that they constitute the most vulnerable social segment. Right to equality, Right against exploitation and Fundamental Right of freedom have enabled the dalits to shed their inferiority tag and stand on an equal footing with the non dalits, greatly enhancing their self respect. The abolition of bonded labour and the Prohibition of Traffic in human beings by the state have come as a huge relief in restoring their dignity and pride. No doubt, the dalit movement regards the constitution as holy cow and any attempt to tamper with it is met with hostility.

All said and done, today there are certain sections of our intelligentsia who feel that time has come for a review of the constitutional provisions. Constitution is not static and has to evolve with the changing times to reflect the changing aspirations of the people. The conditions, prevalent at the time of the framing of the constitution, have changed drastically and our constitution has failed to respond to the environment. Whatever views they may take, the fact remains that the constitution has not failed us; rather it is we who have failed the constitution by interpretations that suit us and our political masters.

Now it is time to shift the radar screen to the graph of the dalit movement post Dr. Ambedkar. His death in 1956 created a void in dalit movement; it seemed to be faltering as the rights, for which it fought, were acceded to by the constitution and it was left directionless. Certain developments took place in the realm of dalit polity which is outlined briefly.

The Republican Party of India (RPI) was formed in Maharashtra to fill the vacuum created by the demise of Ambedkar. At the time of its formation, the RPI opted for collective leadership because there was no acceptable leader in the party who could carry along with him the entire party and reconcile the internal differences. However, soon internal squabbles broke out within the party and accusations started flying thick and fast against each other. Kamble, one of the main leaders of the collegiums, stated that Ambedkarism was all about constitutionalism and only educated people like him could understand it. He denigrated Dadasaheb Gaikwad, the senior leader of the party and ridiculed him for his village attire. He even accused him of colluding with the communists and departing away from the ideology of RPI. One of the remarkable achievements of RPI was to carry out a nationwide Satyagraha related to the land issue under the stewardship of Gaikwad. Alarmed at the increasing political clout of Gaikwad, the Congress leadership of Maharashtra consciously launched its co-optation strategy by making advances towards him. Gaikwad went to the Rajya Sabha with the support of the Congress, thus depriving RPI of its most well known activist/leader. Today, RPI is in shambles and politically, it is not in a position to counter the forces, not well dispossessed towards the dalits. The political movement of the dalits in Maharashtra has been reduced to many factions of RPI, some factions of dalit panthers and numerous other bill board organizations which spring up on the eve of elections to show their relevance and share their claim of political rent from the rulers. Needless to say, all of them swear by Ambedkarism and call themselves Ambedkarites. One faction would align with the Congress, another would pay homage to BJP and another one would be loyal to another party and quite interestingly, all would be Ambedkarites. This is nothing but blatant and naked political opportunism on the part of the dalit parties in Maharashtra.

The Congress emerged stronger to lay claim over the dalit constituency. The dominance of the Congress over the dalit masses was so strong that the dalit movement lost its sting and even an iconic personality like Ambedkar was reduced to mere text books. However, apart from RPI, there were a few sporadic incidents of dalit assertiveness. The most conspicuous event was the formation of the Dalit Panther Party in 1972. The panthers took inspiration directly from the Black Panther Party of United States and took to violent protests and demonstrations, thus lending an element of militancy into the movement. The formation of Dalit Panthers and the corresponding concomitant philosophy marks a basic change in the annals of dalit resistance. The initial indulgence in militancy through the use of rustic arms and threats gave the movement an air of revolutionary tinge with the activists taking to streets on the issue of dalit exploitation/atrocities and often attacking Hindu religion, administrative machinery and police. The movement also boasted of some achievements like forcing the Government of India to fill backlog vacancies of dalits. The age old notion of dalit passiveness was discarded by the birth of this party and dalits developed a sense of security, particularly in the rural areas. The Panthers could not sustain the movement for long. Several reasons could be attributed to this like speaking obscene language at public meetings, propagating the politics of hate and personal vendetta, weak organizational strength with a predominantly urban leadership and its failure to link itself with the ongoing social movements of the time. The leadership failed to come together on a common bandwagon. Raja Dhale was inclined towards Ambedkarism and Buddhism while Namdeo Dhasal showed his drift towards communism. Dhasal believed that the Indian constitution had its own limitations and hence the movement could not be sustained within the democratic sphere. His advocacy for class conflicts brought him into conflict with the Ambedkarites in the party who accused him of being a communist and hence, unfit to carry forward the legacy of Ambedkar. At present, a branch of the dalit panthers is operative in the southern state of Tamil Nadu having truck with the lower caste organizations.

Coming back to the Congress, though Congress publicly professed to be the party of all communities;

its leadership was mostly confined to upper castes and royal family connections/landlords. Lack of inner party democracy, prevalence of dynastic politics both at the centre and states, culture of ideological intolerance of other shades of political opinion, general reduction in the power of regional Congress satraps and the proclivity of the high command of the party to impose its will on the overall party cadre led to the decrease in the pan India appeal of the party. Meanwhile political awareness increased among the dalits and their aspirations went up a notch higher. They were now no longer ready to be looked upon as mere vote banks or passive beneficiaries of state largesse. They wanted a share in power and were convinced that mere tokenism and symbolism of the Congress are not going to help their matters. There was an air of desperation and restlessness among the rank and file of the dalit population. The situation was ripe for the dalit movement to reinvent itself and take a shot at power.

The onset of the Mandal syndrome in polity in the early 1990s altered the ground rules of Indian politics with the backward leaders desperate to take up the reins of power. The backward and the extremely backward sections of the population became conscious of their electoral clout and gradually, the fulcrum of power began to shift away from the upper caste elites. The dalit movement could not afford to screech to a grinding halt and soon the Bahujan Samajwadi Party (BSP) under the leadership of Kanshiram-Mayawati duo came into its elements to create ripples throughout the Hindi heartland. The rise of the BSP marks a watershed in the annals of the dalit polity in the northern part of the country. The party was founded in 1984 and its ambit was enlarged from the dalits to the Bahujan Samaj inclusive of minorities, backwards and the poor. Before forming BSP, Kanshiram had also launched BAMCEF for protecting the interests of government employees, belonging to the backward and the dalit communities. The modus operandi of Kanshiram had nothing to do with Ambedkarism or his policies based on unflinching commitment to principles, ideology and broad human values. He used to say famously that he dealt in people while Ambedkar carried books. He combined history with mythology, without being circumscribed by ideology, displaying both pragmatism and opportunism in the process. Ambedkar talked about the annihilation of castes while Kanshiram contemplated to create caste identity, in order to bring about more effective mobilization of the dalit masses. Kanshiram talked of samtamulak samaj meaning thereby an equal society with all the castes being seen as equal and having their own caste identities.

Ambedkar opined that caste distinctions arose due to Aryan—non Aryan divide, quite in contrast to Kanshiram, who juxtaposed his Bahujan movement with trenchant criticism of Manuwad. For Kanshiram, Manuwad refers to the system under which brahminical superiority was superimposed over that of society, sanctified by Manusmriti and other sacred literature, becoming an instrument for the exploitation and subjugation of the lower caste people.

The growth of BSP has been rather spectacular. In 1993, it aligned with the Samajwadi Party (SP) in Uttar Pradesh and the coalition came to power in the subsequent assembly elections under the chief ministership of Mulayam Singh Yadav. In mid 1995, Mayawati withdrew support from the coalition government and became the Chief Minister of the state with the support of BJP. The then Prime Minister, PV Narsimha Rao described the elevation of Mayawati to the post of chief minister as the miracle of democracy. It was the first time in independent India that a predominantly dalit party secured access to the corridors of power despite several odds. Towards the end of 1995, the BJP withdrew support from her government and fresh elections were held to the state assembly, after a spell of President's rule in the state. The 1997 Assembly Elections resulted into a fractured verdict and a hung assembly. The BSP tied up with the BJP once again, with an understanding to rotate the CM's chair after every 6 months. After completing her rotation, she refused to hand over power to the BJP. The BSP legislature party split and kept a BJP government in power for the next 4 and half years. After the Assembly Elections of 2002, the BSP formed a coalition government with the BJP once again, but this time, with Mayawati as chief minister throughout. In August 2003, this coalition government fell as the BJP withdrew support. In what was viewed as collaboration between the BJP and the SP, the Assembly speaker (belonging to BJP) recognized the split of the BSP legislature party, which allowed Mulayam to become the CM of the state with the support of the rebel group.

In May 2007, the UP state assembly saw the BSP emerging as the single majority party with 207 seats, the first party to do so since 1991. This astounding victory of Mayawati was attributed to her policy of reaching out to the upper castes, which flocked towards her, deserting the Congress and the BJP in the process. It was hailed as a breakthrough in Indian polity because not often, we get to see the exodus of upper castes to join the dalit movement juggernaut. It was not the love for Mayawati that saw the upper castes drifting towards her; rather it was a tactical decision on their part to vote the pro backwards, mandalite party out of power. The BJP and the Congress had ceased to be the effective alternatives to the SP and the common perception among the upper caste population was that only Mayawati can check SP. BSP became the 3rd largest national party with over 10 percent votes across the country.

Unfortunately, the BSP government was swept out of power in the 2012 Assembly Elections in Uttar Pradesh. The anti incumbency factor, corruption charges against the government and the disenchantment of the upper caste constituency led to the decrease of BSP's seats from a high of 207 to a paltry 80 seats. The outreach policy of Mayawati had its limitations; the upper castes had not voted for BSP because of its ideology but it was, in essence, a negative vote to keep SP out. Once the upper castes realized the agenda of the dalit party, they had no compunctions in switching over to the SP in 2012. Apart from UP, the BSP also made electoral forays into states like Punjab, Haryana, Bihar and Madhya Pradesh but failed to make significant strides. States like Punjab, West Bengal, Bihar, Tamil Nadu and Andhra Pradesh despite fair population of scheduled castes have failed to witness an appreciable dalit upsurge. What are the reasons for this? Is the dalit movement losing its sheen or has it reached the plateau, from where the law of diminishing return has set in? Why has the dalit movement not been able to create a pan India appeal? Why is it at cross roads and what are its inherent contradictions? Has it drifted from its original moorings? What should it do to reinvent itself and make itself more relevant?

Dalit Movement: Politics of sectarianism/ negativity/identity/exclusion

Ambedkar had a bitter dislike for the Varna System which he felt was responsible for the creation of a caste based society and the logical outcome of this was the inhuman treatment meted out to the lower castes by the caste Hindus. In his book—Annihilation of Castes—he talked about a society free from the existence of caste because he had the firm conviction that as long as there are castes, there will be outcastes. Hence for him, abolition of caste was an effective way to counter the threats posed by brahminical hegemony. Unfortunately, after the death of Ambedkar, the leaders of the dalit movement made caste a potential tool for mobilizing the lower castes as vote banks. The caste identity feelings were given fillip as this was considered necessary on the road to attainment of political power. Strategically, this caste identity consciousness helped the movement in the short run with BSP able to grab power in Uttar Pradesh, taking advantage of a fractured polity and first past the pole system. But then, this approach has its own limitations. Dalits comprise 16-18 percent population of the entire country. In a diverse multi cultural, multi religious, multi lingual society, the rules of democracy are crystal clear. No movement speaking the language of sectarianism and exclusion can hope to survive in the long run. Even when we look from an electoral perspective, the dalit leadership cannot achieve the critical mass to capture political power until and unless it gets into an electoral understanding with other parties or social groupings. It is the imperative need of the parliamentary democratic model that only those parties/movements gather steam who speak the language of inclusion, cooperation and adjustment and are ready to work and forge alliances with other groupings. The militant posturing and vitriolic hate speeches directed at other social groups are not going to help matters; rather they are going to complicate things. Other social groups/communities start nurturing animosity towards the dalits and increasingly become hostile to them. This is what is happening precisely in Uttar Pradesh where ground level hostilities have flared up between the OBC supporters of SP and dalits of BSP. The forces of dalitisation and mandalisation are often at logger heads with each other. This cycle continues uninterrupted. It is this politics of vendetta and revenge that the dalit activists need to be aware of and for this to happen meaningfully, the dalit movement has no other option but to emphasise on integration and reconciliation.

Kanshiram, a shrewd tactician knew that dalits, on their own, can't capture power and hence, his call for a Bahujan Samaj. Rising on the crest of the Mandal wave and using anti upper caste rhetoric, his goal was the consolidation of the backwards and the dalits as this process would pay rich electoral dividends. He was not wrong. In 1993, a coalition government of SP and BSP came to power. The backwards and the dalits broke the upper caste stranglehold over the power structures. After the tumbling down of this grand social alliance edifice due to the vaunting personal ambitions of Mulayam and Mayawati, BSP did not hesitate to jump on the Hindutva/BJP rath. Mayawati became the CM of UP thrice before 2007 and every time, it was the BJP that was instrumental in making her realize of dreams of power capture. In 2007, she formed her own government but this became possible only when she toned down her anti upper caste rhetoric and tried to enlist their support by reaching out to them. Much to the heart burning of the dalit community, she gave tickets to a large number of Brahmins and Muslims to contest elections. This step ensured a fair percentage of upper caste and Muslim votes to her party.

The dalit intelligentsia has to realize that the demographic composition of UP is such that the dalit leadership cannot be expected to get more than 80-100 seats by itself, even if the entire dalit population goes along with it. The dalit agenda has to be inclusive if it wants power. The dalit leadership may lament the doing away of Separate Electorates, a concept very close to the heart of Ambedkar but then, they should not feel cheated as, in place of Separate Electorates, the concept of reservation has been put into vogue. The Joint Electorate system places premium on a society that is India, unlike Separate Electorates that create a society that is dalit. Ambedkar never accepted that India is a nation in the early phase of his struggle against brahminical hegemony. According to him, we are inhabited by a plethora of castes/communities and all these castes/communities constitute distinct nationalities. We can't blame him for this thinking. Nation, as a concept, means a geographical entity inhabited by people who speak the same language, share the same culture and consider themselves to be part of the nation on the basis of this common bonding. A nation shows strong unifying tendencies and does away with the centrifugal forces. India, on the contrast, is a vast geographical stretch, populated by a huge population of different ethnic strands, speaking multiple languages, having varied cultures and religions and of course, don't forget the plethora of castes and communities within each religion. Indians tend to give more importance to family, kinship and society in comparison to the state. Hatred towards the colonial regime was perhaps the only cementing factor that brought together various cross sections of the population of the country in their fight against the British. Under the influence of western education and evolving political thoughts on nation-state, the national leadership of the time decided to unify the entire Indian landscape politically though there were perils involved in the process. The irony is—Ambedkar presided over the making of the nation with his vision and constitution. According to an article in one of the leading dailies of the country—we are living in a society that is increasingly, getting intolerant and the general proclivity seems to paint everything in white and black, oblivious to the fact that in between black and white, there is another shade i.e. grey. It is in this grey zone that a common ground can be found. This is where the dalit leadership has to fill in.

According to Ambedkar, the greatest threat to the working of our democracy emanates from three factors—hero worship, incongruence of political democracy with the needs of the socio economic democracy and constitutional anarchy. The dalit movement of today is enmeshed in the very vices from which Ambedkar sought to insulate it. It has become a fashion among the dalit activists to indulge in a virulent denigrating campaign against the national icons of the stature of MK Gandhi and Nehru; at times, mudslinging and calling names are no taboos. There are some intellectuals for whom Ambedkar is a bread and butter issue and hence, most of their energies are spent in trying to prove that Ambedkar was greater than Gandhi and in doing so, they elevate Ambedkar to the status of godhood. Not only this, the very name of Ambedkar for them is such that it arouses them in agitation mood at the drop of a hat. The Ambedkar-Nehru cartoon which appeared in a NCERT textbook, though innocuous, was enough to incite them and things took such a turn that the Thorat Committee has called for the removal of many so called offensive cartoons pertaining to depiction of politicians and bureaucrats in poor light. **The dalit activists/intelligentsia behave as if Ambedkar is their property and they hold patent rights over him. In doing so, they diminish the stature of Ambedkar and the impression that he was a leader only of the dalits gains ground. Do the dalit activists have to be reminded that Ambedkar was a national icon?** The fact remains that Ambedkar was very much a human being and a politician like Gandhi and other nationalist leaders of the time. He had his share of differences with Gandhi and others but differences are very much a part and parcel of democracy and have to be fought with logic, rather than resorting to histrionics. Cartoons are an integral part of academic/intellectual discourse and there is hardly any prominent leader on whom a cartoon has not been made. Our own Nehru was known to be a great admirer of cartoons, especially those sketched by Shankar.

Ambedkar's life was based on values, principles and a strong commitment to the tenets of democracy. Dissent and divergence of opinion to him, were integral parts of democracy. Dissent, if suppressed, would stifle democracy. A vibrant engagement in debates and discussions is what constitutes the lifeline to democracy. Ambedkar would certainly have been horrified if he were alive and had the chance to witness his so called supporters making a mountain out of a mole hill. Denigration of leaders of other communities and the tendency to get provoked without adequate reason, on imaginary threats to the dalit icons, may pit the dalits to the ire of other communities. Remember how the remarks of Mayawati directed at Mahatma Gandhi triggered a controversy and caused furore nationwide. The dalit leadership/intelligentsia must respect the non dalit icons also and not make crude attempts to rediscover Ambedkar to suit their narrow sectarian agendas. Gandhi was as great as Ambedkar and attempts to compare the two in bad light, should be avoided. The requirements of a plural, inclusive democracy mandate that divergence of opinions should not lead to shrill war tantrums, with the rules implying strict adherence to conductance of civil mannerisms and tolerance of different shades of opinions. The immense contribution of Ambedkar to the dalit and national causes is beyond doubt but can the nation afford to let dalit activists hurl abuses at Gandhi and other great national leaders. Can the nation overlook the work done by Gandhi in dalit inhabited areas, his efforts at removal of untouchability and caste based discrimination? This was done at a time when there was no constitution to safeguard the interests of dalits and the overall Hindu society was highly orthodox and differentiated. Mahatma's endorsement of temple entry programmes and access to public places led to a lot of hue and cry and he was vociferously resisted by the caste Hindus. At times, some Congress leaders complained that the Mahatma was too warped up in Harijan welfare work and he did not care an iota whether they lived or died, whether they were bonded or free. Gandhi emphasized on the dignity of labour and was of the opinion that doing service to the community should form an intrinsic part of any educational curriculum. Alas! The armchair Ambedkarites of today can't understand this.

Ambedkar's criticism of Gandhi had nothing to do with the emancipation of dalits, rather it was sheer politics. Gandhi took strong exception to Ambedkar's claim of being the sole dalit spokesman as he felt that he spoke for all the Indians, including dalits. Politically, Ambedkar had to counter Gandhi and hence, his stringent criticism of Gandhi. The Mahatma had his differences with Jinnah, the RSS, and the communists and even within the Congress but such incidents can't take credit away from his crusade against the forces of colonialism and imperialism. Unlike Ambedkar, Gandhi was not solely blinded by the dalit cause as he had to take along with him all shades of opinion and people—dalits, caste Hindus, Muslims, socialists, communists etc. Hence he had to adopt a cautious approach to the dalit cause, a fact which Ambedkar construed to be deliberate dilly dallying.

The dalit movement has to realize that upgrading Ambedkar to the status of God would lead to his seclusion from the critical academic world and denial of chance to the future generations to examine him from a neutral perspective. This is a huge loss to the movement which, without serious introspection, would refuse to transform itself into a more viable and potent entity resulting in redundancy. There should be space for criticism in democracy. The moment it is curbed, fresh flow of ideas would stop and the movement runs the risk of becoming opaque and outdated. Politics of hate has its limitations while politics of whine leads to ridicule. The joint electorate system has tied down the dalit representatives with the requirements of whip and party line and hence, exclusive dalit agenda can't be carried out by them.

Politics of identity has its own shortfalls. The dalit leadership/intelligentsia feel that the institution of caste and the resulting caste solidarity would elevate them to seats of power and lead to flow of more funds and positive affirmative programmes to their constituency. The protagonists of the dalit movement tend to glorify their identity, citing examples from our history and our heritage. At times, references are also made to mythological figures to buttress their positions. Then the carefully created identity is brought into conflict with other parallel identities and the confrontation between rival communities start surfacing. The mobilization/consolidation phase commences. The subscribers of identity politics utilize the power of myth, cultural symbols and kinship relations to mould the feelings of a shared community and politicize these aspects to claim recognition for their particular identities. However, does the issue of identity politics work that way? **The fact is that Indians carry multiple**

identities which may be casteist, linguistic, religious, regional or any other. During the time of elections, depending upon the wave and circumstances, there is interplay of different types of identities and it becomes very difficult to conjecture which identity will prevail and fetch votes. Despite the prevalence of the mandalisation wave in the better part of the nineties based on backward caste mobilization, the rise of the rightwing Hindutva identity could not be checked. The religious identity prevailed over the caste identity. The Dravida movement, way down into the south, was basically not only about non Brahmin caste empowerment but it also talked about a separate linguistic identity as manifested in its anti Hindi agitation. It talked about its distinct cultural identity as opposed to the Aryans. Given the diverse nature of Indian population, a candidate of any political party has to form a coalition that cuts across caste, religious and ethnic diversities to have any realistic chances of winning. This necessitates compromise. Lastly but not the least, identity factor seems to work more at the local regional level. The Muslims of Uttar Pradesh and West Bengal may have the same religious identity but when it comes to linguistic identity, they speak Hindi and Bengali respectively. The Muslims of Bengal or Tamil Nadu may not identify themselves with the language of Hindi as the UP Muslims do. Political parties speak about granting official recognition to Urdu as the Second Language of the state but the question is—is this identifying language of the Indian Muslims? Merely recognizing Urdu won't fetch you the Muslim votes as majority of that population in Tamil Nadu or Bengal or say, Assam speak regional languages of those states. The dalits of Bihar may have the same caste identity as the dalits of UP, but they are more likely to vote for a Nitish Kumar, than say Mayawati who also belongs to the dalit group. Hence despite being a strong votary of caste identity politics, the dalit movement has failed to have a pan India appeal, leave alone the capture of power. When the voting pattern is examined, it becomes clear that it's not only the caste identity that matters but voter preference is also determined by a plethora of identity markers like religion, ethnicity, regionalism, language and others. Add to these identity parameters, the issues related to development, welfare of the people and governance and the scenario becomes muddied and complicated. So, for how long the dalit movement or even the Mandal movement keep the caste identity tag pasted on their heads; it will be interesting to watch?

In the post Ambedkar era, the dalit upsurge has not been witnessed, barring some exceptions as in the most populous state of UP. In this state, the factor that led to dalit visibility was not the philosophy of Ambedkar or the triumph of Ambedkarism but it was due to the large population of a particular dalit community to which Mayawati belongs or due to the support of social groups that originally were not part of the dalit scheme of things. No doubt, realizing her political compulsions, she opted for a grand social alliance, a possible replication of the Congress in its heydays but then, what happened afterwards? Induction of outsiders i.e. the non dalits in the party ranks led to the dilution of the core Bahujan ideology. Rifts opened between the dalits and their leaders. The dalit population became suspicious of the intentions of the outsiders and as a matter of fact, never accepted them. This had a de motivating impact on the movement and overall, it was weakened.

The growth of the movement appears to have been arrested by its negativism. The actual Ambedkar has never been deciphered and crude attempts have been made to dwarf him by projecting him as a disgruntled casteist whose sole obsession seemed to be securing reservation for the dalits and lambasting the hegemony of the Brahminical system. Only his differences with the Congress leaders have been highlighted and perverted attempts have been made to paint the Congress leaders as anti dalit and votaries of caste prejudices. The fact of Ambedkar being a true humanist and democrat was very reluctantly brought to the fore. His championing of the cause of women in the Hindu Code Bill remains largely unnoticed. He formed the Indian Labour Party and the Indian Republican Party and at no point of time, he was solely glued to caste.

He called for the annihilation of caste; it's another matter that his followers of later years based their political stake on caste. Ambedkarism has just been used in furtherance of their political agendas and as a tool to hit at others. Whether it is the appearance of Ambedkar's cartoons in NCERT text books or the publication of the book—Worshipping False Gods—on Ambedkar, the reaction of the dalit activists has been kneejerk and incoherent. Rather than countering the perceived insult to Ambedkar with logic and sound arguments, they take to streets and vandalism raising shrill war cry. The dalit elites, the so called followers of Ambedkar want to exercise monopolistic control over the movement and are hesitant to bring the poorer dalit masses into the leadership fold. They have their own agendas which they want to impose on the overall movement. This perhaps is the reason for the slowing down of the growth process of the movement. Ambedkarism for this class is a mere instrument or slogan to fulfill their nefarious designs of maintaining their supremacy among dalit ranks and simultaneously, they also indulge in vituperative attacks on the non dalits for past atrocities. Interestingly, they tend to forget that today; we are living in the 21st century. The reasons for this are not difficult to surmise. It suits their agenda of keeping the ordinary dalit masses ghettoized, excluded and segregated from the national mainstream. This act of the movement is a disservice to the cause of national reconciliation and nation building. It is a pity that the dalit vision of fighting hegemony is becoming murkier because in the process, a section of the elite dalits has hegemonised power itself.

Agitations and protests on the streets for Ambedkar were the grammar of anarchy and it is precisely this anarchy into which the dalit leadership is plummeting. Rather than entering into a dialogue with the government and other stakeholders of our democracy in a meaningful way, it has resorted to brinkmanship. Its energy has been wasted in organizing protests on issues that do not have any bearing on the poor rural dalits and have more to do to mere tokenism or symbolism. **To its credit, it can be said that the dalit activists have graduated as a powerful pressure group in the country and the situation as of now is that no political party is in a position to ignore them. Despite more than 60 years of reservation and the loopholes present in it, the political class is avoiding**

a debate on it for fear of appearing politically incorrect. Damage to a Mayawati statue in UP was repaired within no time for fear of a dalit backlash by the SP Government. In Mumbai, Indu Mills Area has been taken over by the dalit activists for building Ambedkar statue. Quite amusingly, the Shiv Sena wants the statue of Balasaheb Thackeray to be built there. The state government which is a coalition of Congress and NCP is helpless and is hardly in a position to stall the building of Ambedkar statue. And now, it is learnt that the Centre has Okayed the proposal to build the Ambedkar memorial at that site. RSS, once a staunch opposer of reservation for dalits in public employment now appears to be singing a different tune. Recently, Asish Nandy, the famous sociologist had to bear the brunt of dalit fury for his comments about high corruption levels among dalits and backwards. The dalit activists called for his arrest and invoking SC/ST Act against him. Now, coming back to the moot point—is open display of such intimidation and pressure tactics desirable in democracy? Instead of patting their backs, the dalit activists must understand that a possible counterattack may be launched on them. Just see the recent incidents of violent clashes between the dalits and the backwards in Tamil Nadu and UP. The Samajwadi party's open stand against the provision of reservation in promotion in government jobs, the DMK's indifference towards it and the stalling of the Reservation in Promotion Bill in the House are incidents that point to fault lines existing between the dalits and the backwards. Moreover, the common dalits are not being benefitted and their quality of life remains miserable despite such fire and brimstone from the dalit leadership/intelligentsia/activists on the streets.

One of the most glaring drawbacks of the dalit movement is that it has not been able to free itself from the shackles of past history and continue to parrot the acts of past atrocities and caste violence perpetrated on them by the caste Hindus. At a time when majority of our population is young and more than 65 percent of our population is below 35 years of age, it is quite natural that they are not bogged down by history. The young generation dalits should look ahead and not backwards like their predecessors shedding tears for past injustices heaped on them and that too, in a country that prides itself on Ambedkar's constitution and not Manusmriti. By referring constantly to past, is the dalit movement not guilty of preparing the ground for politics of hatred and vendetta, rather than speaking the language of reconciliation? By demanding concessions due to being historically wronged, is the dalit movement not guilty of asking for price extraction based on victimhood? Isn't it resorting to blackmail of the system for its benefits? It continues to play the victim card unabashedly and put pressure on the polity. **The final call has to be taken by it—does it have faith in the concept of democratic welfare state as envisaged by Ambedkar, leading to a more equal, egalitarian and inclusive society or does it intend to reverse the past discriminations, rather than undoing them?** Just consider the statement of the dalit icon, Kanshiram—we will give reservation to the upper castes. The initial bitterness of the dalits was understandable but the fact that this bitterness is being relayed to future generations is a cause for concern. This casts doubts towards the very intentions of the movement. Is it going to extricate itself from politics of hate and revenge to submerge into the national mainstream? This constitutes a challenge to its leadership and the forth coming trends will be keenly watched by students of Indian polity.

Ambedkar stood for rationality and denounced the socially stratified brahminical system based on logic and conviction. On the other hand, his followers lampoon the system just for the sake of rhetoric and constituency cultivation. Their obsession with Manusmriti and attacks on Hindu gods and goddesses take a perverted form, in the process drawing them away from the non dalits and inviting their ire needlessly. What's remarkable is the fact that most of these dalit activists visit Hindu temples and worship Hindu deities and practice Hindu rituals. There is a wide chasm between what they preach and what they practice. It is this dual behavior norm that is eating into the very vitals of the movement and subjecting it to mockery and ridicule. The dalit leadership continues to highlight the prevalent caste distinctions in Hinduism but when it comes to caste schisms in Islam and Christianity, it maintains a studied silence. The dalit Christians are so much victims of caste oppression of upper caste Christians as the dalits in Hindu religion. The movement's claim of being progressive cannot be sustained on the basis of selective criticism of some religions and being silent and indifferent towards other religions.

Talking about identity, at times the identity obsession of the dalits assume ludicrous proportions. The dalit intelligentsia believes that only it is tasked with the responsibility of speaking on behalf of the dalit constituency. Even the genuine pro dalit concerns of the non dalits are looked at with suspicion and uneasiness. The feeling of insecurity complex is still there and faith in itself seems to be lacking. Even the great Ambedkar fumed when Gandhi took up the Harijan welfare work. This "I know best attitude of the movement acts as an obstacle to serious self introspection and course correction when needed. Identity factor has its own limitations. If a non dalit cannot speak for a dalit, why should a balmiki speak for a paswan? Taking the same logic of the movement forward, why should a dalit man speak for a dalit woman? The harsh reality is that identity has no single variable but is associated with many variables.

Apart from the intellectuals, political leaders and the dalit elites, the dalit movement has another component i.e. the nongovernmental organizations. These groups are not guided by any overriding philosophy of dalit concern. They take up a bundle of individual cases and weep all the time when atrocities on dalits are committed. Of late, some sections of the media have also fallen prey to the phenomenon. What are the common dalits going to achieve out of all these acts? Non dalits are also being killed, raped and maimed. Why is the spotlight only on dalits? Is it out of genuine concern or a mere vote bank calculation? Law and order is in poor shape in most of the Indian states with the victims belonging to both the dalits and the non dalits. Why should there be any politics on victimhood? The life of a non dalit is as precious as the life of a dalit. No movement can succeed without a philosophy and there would be no support for philosophy until and unless, it is internalized and popularized. Rather than sloganeering and demonstrating on the streets, the dalit movement must provide alternatives to the people. Making suggestions to improve the dalit conditions should be the norm, indulgence in criticism should be the exception.

Dalit movement shares a broad concern for asserting dalit rights to life, livelihood, dignity and the process of democratization. However, the post Ambedkar era has not been a spectator to any principled and ideological stand of the movement in the realm of dalit emancipation and at times, it gets stuck in factionalism with all the splinter groups claiming to represent the true Ambedkarian legacy. The BSP may have captured power in the state of UP but its rise has been made possible through opportunistic alliances with parties or social groups that have nothing to do with the thoughts or ideology of Ambedkar. The leadership remained cut off from the masses and apart from acts of symbolism and patronage to some extent, has never endeavoured to understand the dalit aspirations. In the states of West Bengal and Kerala, the upsurge of the lower castes has remained a pipe dream. Considering the fact that both of these states were under communist rule for a considerable period of time in post independent India, the inherent perceived dichotomy between class and caste did not work to the advantage of the dalits. The communists kept the institution of caste at bay and took to mobilization on class lines defeating the caste plank of the dalits. Punjab, Haryana, Bihar and Tamil Nadu have a substantial dalit population but internal rivalries between the competing dalit sub castes have not done anything to the cause of the movement. In the states of Gujarat, Chattisgarh and MP, the

Hindutva forces are posing a threat to the movement and as reports pour out, the dalits are being Hinduised and encouraged to join the Hindutva fold. At present, there isn't something like a pan India dalit movement. The dalits are evenly dispersed throughout the country and though there may be some mobilization among them on some burning issue, the impact is generally localized and fails to have a spill over impact in the rest of the country. The movement has failed to articulate the aspirations of the dalit masses in tune with the fast changing socio political landscape of the country.

The national economy is integrating with the global economy, the national boundaries of nations are becoming porous with increased interflows of capital, technology and highly skilled human personnel but despite this, the dalit movement has failed to develop an economic perspective. It has failed to integrate the aspirations of the dalit youth with the rest of the youth population to take full advantage of the opportunities that globalization has offered. Apart from its oft repeated demand for reservation in private sector, it cannot think of any other alternative. Its agenda continues to be determined by the urban elites who have no ears for the rural dalit masses. **Even though reservation benefits have not percolated to the bottom strata of the dalit population and only 10-20 percent of the already well off sections among them corner majority of the benefits, the dalit leadership/ intelligentsia continues to regard it as the instrument of dalit emancipation showing its complete oblivion from the harsh ground level realities.** The movement has no answers to the adverse implications of the forces of globalization on the life of an ordinary dalit.

The agrarian sphere is witness to changing socio economic dynamics; the so called land reforms have failed to ameliorate the plight of majority of dalits who are landless and social tensions between the landed class and the dalits are not acts of aberration. Despite the gravity of the situation, the leadership is happy to keep itself aloof and concentrate on the reservation demand for the urban dalits or take to the streets on any matter connected to the perceived insult to dalit icons. Its attitude towards the dalit cause is superficial and apart from incoherent actions that are aimed at playing to the gallery, it lacks a proper and well crafted strategy to counter the emergent community problems. To any commoner or lay man, the elite dalit attitude appears to be one that is solely concerned with its self aggrandizement, manned by self seeking dalit leaders whose interest lies in keeping a common dalit ignorant and ghettoized. The movement must respond to the aspirations and demands of the common dalit masses otherwise it risks alienation.

To survive in the long run, a movement should not focus on short term gains; it should not confine itself to ivory towers and must be willing to not only influence the general mood but also get influenced by it so as to have a feel of the pulse of the population. It is very much an organic entity which has to survive and evolve in an environment that gets affected by several variables like political, economic, social etc. and for this to happen, it is essential for it to get periodic feedback from the ground level workers from which it derives its strength. This prevents it from going into a rut.

The dalit movement has set its target of attaining political power because the real key to power lies in the political executive. The political executive can alter the prevailing social dynamics and steer the pace of social reforms. **It is no doubt a sound argument but what is strange is that capture of political power has become an end in itself for the dalit leadership and the dalit emancipation project has been relegated to the background.** Dalits have become ministers and chief ministers but once in power, they have displayed the same traits and attitudes that are very much reminiscent of the upper caste elites. The principles underlying the movement have been thrown to the winds and in the name of political pragmatism, they are not averse to joining hands with the rightists, the leftists, the communists or the mandalites who, in essence, have nothing to do with the overall dalit ideology. This is sheer political opportunism and bankruptcy as though the short term gains are visible, in the long run, the movement finds itself weakened. In real terms, there never has been a pan India dalit party post independence and today, barring Mayawati to some extent, there is hardly any dalit leader who is a worthy successor to Ambedkar and has all India acceptability. The dalit leaders are present in all the parties but then, the control of the party high command is immense and it is not uncommon to find divergence of opinions on matters where a united front should have been presented. This is a huge setback to the movement.

Dalits do not constitute a homogeneous unit and are differentiated into hundreds of sub castes with each of them having their own distinct occupations, customs and histories. These sub castes avoid inter dinning and inter marriages among themselves and have their own hierarchy in the social scheme of things. Some of these sub castes have been left out of the state induced development process of the dalits while the dominant ones have taken full advantage of reservation and state affirmative action programmes and climbed up the social ladder. Naturally the deprived dalit sub castes are feeling let down and there are clamours for sub reservation for them within the prescribed 15 percent ceiling for the dalits. The dalit leadership has failed to see the writing on wall and has not so far initiated any worthwhile step to resolve the inner conflict. If they fail to do so, other political parties may start taking advantage of the situation and allure the dissatisfied sub castes to their respective camps, making a mockery of the painfully created dalit solidarity. The days of the dalit movement will end and in all probability be replaced by a Bhangi movement, a jatav movement or a madiga movement.

It is not to say that the dalit movement has no credits to its side. Since colonial days, it has played a stellar role in awakening the conscience of the nation to the hapless plight of the dalits and increased their visibility in public places where earlier, they were conspicuous by their absence. Dalits are present in legislatures, administration and other public institutions in the realm of governance. Legislative measures have been adopted to prevent caste based discriminatory practices. The dalit pressure has forced governments to listen to them and at times, even backtrack from decisions that have already been taken by them. However, the material conditions of the majority of dalits have not improved and the process of socio economic empowerment is far from over.

The movement suffers from hallucinations. Ask any dalit leader or an intellectual of dalit studies on the most pressing problem confronting the dalits. The answer will be on predictable lines i.e. the challenge posed by the manuwadis and the brahminical upper castes. You watch any channel—the dalit elite participants in the panel discussion—will never disappoint you. They would keep ranting about the evils perpetrated by the manuwadis and the historical atrocities suffered by them. You ask them why dalits are in distress and they will blame the brahminical system for it. You talk to them about dalit culture and their answers will be a foregone conclusion; dalit culture was deliberately destroyed by the brahminical culture. All the problems associated with the dalits will be attributed to the devious machinations of the upper castes. This predilection of the dalit movement of putting the blame on others for its gross failures will not depict it in good light. Of course, there may be some truth in what they are saying but putting the onus solely on outsiders will prevent the movement from looking inwards and going for remedial measures when needed. The so called manuwadis have vanished long back and whether the dalits realize this or not, the fact is that the mandalites have become their real challengers in the present day Indian polity. It's time the movement breaks away from the past and focus on issues that have relevance today.

Now let's turn to the dalit elites/intelligentsia. They keep themselves enmeshed in useless discussions from which the common dalits are not going to gain anything. Just consider and think about the ranging debates among them. Who are the dalits? Are they having different origin from the Shudras? How did the caste system originate? Were the dalits followers of Buddha? What wrongs were committed by Nehru? Was Mahatma Gandhi anti dalit? Was Ambedkar superior to Gandhi? Did Gandhi blackmail Ambedkar on Poona Pact? These debates are engendered not out of any real academic initiative or quest but to enable them to run their political shops, to seek rent from certain vested interests and keep the dalit masses aloof from the national mainstream. Taking into account the media's tendency to give space to spicy news for boosting their TRP, some of these debates occasionally find way to newsrooms and television studios and this publicity starved intelligentsia goes gaga over it. Rather than wasting time on these futile debates, the focus of their discourses should be on real ground level facts, the contemporary developments in the nation and around the world and how the marginalized dalits would benefit out of this. Why is that most of the dalit intelligentsia is silent on issues relating to the widespread landlessness of the dalits despite 50 years of the avowed policy of land reforms of state governments and the union government? How capitalism is shaping the world and how is it impinging on the lives of ordinary dalit masses? How the neo economic mantra is leading to a reduction in the public employment opportunities for dalits? Does the dalit movement foresee any role for itself at the time when the forces of neo liberalization are plundering the scarce resources of the country in the name of development? Where does the movement stand in terms of accomplishments when we compare it with the black civil movement of the United States? Does the movement need to understand

and connect with different movements related to the oppressed people throughout the world?

Challenge lies in extricating the movement from past fossilization to the present and then carrying it forward to the future. Then only will it realize what changes have occurred in the caste system in the past hundred years and the anti caste movements have been able to achieve in the realm of social revolution during this period. The entire societal configurations have witnessed transformation while the movement has remained buried in the past. The Dravidian movement of the south in the 1940s and 1950s and the mandalisation of the polity post 1990 in the north have led to the socio political ascendancy of the backward castes. The backward/intermediate castes have consolidated and have become the landed class. Their treatment of the dalit labourers and peasants is no better than the manuwadis. How are capitalism and urbanization threatening to free the society from the tentacles of casteism? How the adoption of Panchayati Raj Act and the government flagship welfare programmes in the rural areas are threatening to reduce the social clout of rural farming elites?

The dalit movement has to engage in a lot of soul searching to find out what it precisely wants and what the goal of the movement is. Does it want to annihilate the institution of caste or does it want to go for aggressive mobilization of the caste plank to become the ruling caste? Since the dalits lack homogeneity and are broken up into several castes and sub castes, which caste/sub caste within the dalit community should rule? If the dalits were to become the ruling caste, then how do we reconstruct the word dalit? The debate does not end here but becomes more open ended and raises several pertinent questions about the real intentions of the movement. **If the dalits suffered immensely due to caste system, then why are they not ready to dispense with it? Why are they still clamouring for caste based preferences? Why do the dalit leaders and intelligentsia tend to view everything through the prism of caste? Why are they organizing rallies based on caste?** Recently the Allahabad High Court has banned the organizing of caste rallies in the state of UP because in its opinion, the caste rallies were the breeding grounds for fomenting animosity between rival communities. They have become platforms of vituperative diatribe of any community against the other. This decision of the judiciary may be debatable, but rather than going into the technical aspects of the decision, if we examine the ground realities, the intention of the court is laudable. **Too much emphasis on caste on the part of dalit leadership/activists makes one wonder whether they want to reverse the clock of discrimination or derive sadist pleasure of seeing the non dalits facing the same music which they did for centuries. Is the movement nursing vendetta feelings towards the non dalits?** The one phenomenon that is currently posing a serious threat to law and order and tending to subvert the process of rule of law is the khap panchayats or the caste panchayats that have sprung up in several parts of western UP and Haryana. The caste panchayats talk about the honour of their castes and very often, these patriarchal bodies do not leave any stone unturned in restricting the mobility and autonomy of their women. Love marriages are a taboo between youths of the dalit and the farming communities. **The fundamental lacuna in the mindset of the movement is that it has failed to comprehend that caste cannot be the source of integration or say, the unifying factor. Castes do not operate on horizontal coordinates, it creates hierarchy. Hierarchy gives oxygen to caste and creates inter and intra caste conflicts.** The dalit emancipation project envisages ushering in of social revolution to bring radical changes in the society. The social revolution entails fighting the caste inequalities and menace, abolish the brahminical hierarchal system and go for a structure that places castes horizontally, rather than vertically. The dalits can take a leaf out of the Dravidian movement whose first priority was to challenge the brahminical superiority and alter the social structure. This was followed by a mass uprising of the non Brahmin castes, the mobilization and consolidation of which, saw the capture of political power by the Dravidian parties. The case of the dalit movement is just diametrically opposite to the Dravidian movement. Capture of political power is more important to it than the carrying out of social revolution as it aims to invert the social pyramid from the corridors of power rather than dismantling the evils of society through the force of the movement. In its quest for power, it has compromised on its ideology resulting in the lack of binding factor and cohesion in the organization. The ground for the mass peoples' movement that can facilitate the takeover of power has not been prepared and this has proved detrimental to the dalit cause.

One major problem with the movement is that it faces an acute leadership crisis and the problem gets accentuated when confronted with the harsh reality of fragmentation of their monolithic entity and the inbuilt ideological incoherence. Rather than having acceptability among all the sections of the dalits, the post independence dalit leadership has limited social support. A Mayawati is considered the tallest dalit leader in the country at present but when we consider her influence, it seems that it is a particular dominant dalit constituency that provides her the votes while less known dalit sub castes are detached from her. In Bihar, there are several dalit sub castes but rather than going with Ram Vilas Paswan, the mahadalits prefer to vote for a Nitish. Apart from the paswans, Ram Vilas's appeal among the other dalit sub castes is limited. Apart from this, the few dalit parties that are visible are leader centric and their electoral fortunes oscillate according to the increase or decrease of the charisma of their leadership, not according to the programmes and policies. If the leaders become opportunistic, the movement loses steam. The second rung leadership is often missing in these parties and the party structure is centralized so much so that at times, it appears that the parties are run on the whims and fancies of their leaders. To be fair to the dalit movement, this phenomenon of complete dominance of individuals on the party structures or say, individuals becoming parties on to themselves is quite common in our polity. Can you imagine a Congress without the Gandhi family or a SP without Mulayam's family? Can DMK survive without Karunanidhi clan or can you dissociate Mamata from Trinamool Congress? So if dalit parties like BSP banks on Mayawati, eyebrows should not be raised; rather the feudality or the dynastic influence that is invading Indian polity needs to be questioned. The internal democracy is missing in most of the parties, the party members are not allowed to speak their minds out and are often, coerced to follow the party line and internal party elections are mere dramas enacted for public consumption and to escape from the gaze of the Election Commission.

Another fact that deserves mention is that the post independent dalit leadership has not grown out of any mass movement but seems to have feudal roots. This, perhaps, explains its detachment from the common dalit masses. Moreover, the lack of internal democracy in these dalit parties like BSP feeds internal dissensions and hence, there is lack of cohesion in the organizations. The opposite may also happen as can be seen in the case of BSP where the party becomes subservient to an individual and the party rank and file does not hesitate to pay obeisance to the leader whose diktats cannot be ignored. The ideological glue that used to bind together the dalit parties has been replaced by opportunism. The ideology has become vague as can be seen in the lack of any economic programme or vision on the part of the dalit movement to address the concerns of the common dalit masses. Most dalit leaderships look for sponsorships from the wealthy and rich non dalit sources. Electioneering and party organization works need huge amounts of funds which can't come from the party workers and hence, it is not rare to find them drifting towards the corporate. Naturally such leaderships can't turn a blind eye towards their donors and do lobbying for them whenever required. Not only this, the infiltration of non dalit interests with big purses in the dalit capture of power in a state led to feelings of being outsiders in their own backyard among the ordinary dalit masses. Being a part of the inclusive Indian democracy, the leadership can't appear to be biased towards their communities to the people at large. They need votes from other social groupings and hence, the dalit agenda recedes further.

The state seeks status quo. The state is the source of authority and can do numerous things but all have to be in the framework of the current order. So, at best the dalit leadership can obtain only certain concessions from the state within the current order and that too, without antagonizing the other social groupings. The present state structure has not responded to them adequately as can be amply demonstrated by the experience of past six decades of utter non espousal of dalit concerns in policy formulation. What the dalits desperately need is the change in the structure of the state that lives up to their expectations. Though Ambedkar believed in state and constitutionalism, his concept of state was such a structure that took notice of the plight of the vulnerable social groups and guaranteed social justice and facilitated in the creation of a just, equal and egalitarian society.

Impact of middle class uprising on dalit movement

Though devoid of Ambedkar's ideals, at times the dalit activists and intelligentsia fall back on Ambedkar to question the rationale of mass secular movements and contemplate to alienate it from the ordinary dalit masses. Anna's crusade against corruption and the mass participation of the middle class in favour of the Jan Lok Pal Bill drew the ire of the dalit leadership/ activists who felt that this uprising was the handiwork of the same classes who were opposed to reservation. Though some utterances of the Anna camp, disparaging the elected representatives, lampooning the parliament and displaying rigidity of stand while debating for the enactment of their own version of the bill were certainly not in good taste, the conclusion of the dalit activists that this middle class uprising threatens Ambedkar's constitution was in fact farfetched and lacked logic. The middle class movement was termed as upper caste movement which was antagonistic to dalit interests. Some of the overzealous and enthusiastic leading lights of the dalit movement went on to advance the argument that Anna's Jan Lok Pal Bill would be detrimental to dalits and open the floodgates of their constant harassments. How ludicrous were their arguments? A secular campaign, a mass movement against the rising tide of corruption was termed as anti dalit. Are the dalits insulated from the very vices of corruption?

Do the evils of corruption not affect the daily lives of people, not sparing the dalits but including them, right from the time of getting their wards admitted in schools to getting birth certificates and even death certificates to inclusion in the BPL category to getting old age pensions and finally to getting themselves admitted to public hospitals? Are the dalits immune from corruption since the dalit intelligentsia/leadership consider themselves to be a different people, coming from a different planet and having their different set of problems and priorities? The answer is a big no; then what makes the dalit movement sing a different tune on these occasions? As one goes up the hierarchy—top policy makers, top bureaucrats, the corporate honchos, the middlemen—the corruption levels keep ballooning. Are the secular national concerns, not the concerns of the dalits? Yes, they are and they should be but the problem with dalit activists/leaders/intelligentsia today is that they have no hesitation in accepting scam tainted leaders as long as these leaders keep shouting the mantra of social justice or say, reservation. **Social justice seems to have become the safe haven to casteist forces having limited vision. The same is true for both the dalit leadership and the mandalites.** Corruption and bad governance are issues that are not on the radar screen of these subaltern movements because they are not related specifically to them but affect the entire population. But the fact remains that the dalits and the extreme backward castes face maximum hardships in a corrupt set up where all your works depend on speed money. The upper affluent class enjoys a working relationship with the politicians and the bureaucrats because they can afford to grease their palms directly or indirectly, something which is out of bonds for the vulnerable disadvantaged population.

Coming back to the moot point, why is the dalit leadership not comfortable with the middle class uprising as was evident during the Anna campaign? Let us contemplate to get to the root of the problem. The phase of dalit assertion in Indian polity was followed by the assertion of the backward classes. Now, we are looking at the prospects of a new assertion and this assertion is of the middle classes which has the potential to bring about wide ranging changes in the realm of Indian polity. Unlike the previous assertions of the dalits and the backwards, the middle class assertion is not based on narrow considerations of identity and caste but is more catholic and secular. Its vision is also diametrically opposite from that of the dalit/backward constituencies. It does not seek favours from the state on caste and community lines but raises questions that are national concerns like rampant corruption existing in our system, the rising incidences of social crimes like the one in New Delhi on the horrific gang rape of a young paramedical student, the issue of deficit in governance and the issue of adoption of pro people approach in this age of predatory capitalism. Its target constituency is not determined according to castes and religions. The middle class talks about the problems facing the common people, the working people and the professionals. What does it show? This section of the population is more class conscious and this is something with which the dalit intelligentsia/leadership is not expected to agree as even today, it feels that caste determines class. Class can't be seen in isolation from caste.

The arrival of middle class marks the arrival of new India. The ushering in of liberalization post 1990s created opportunities and gave wings to the aspirations of middle class to swim with the global tide. The mandalisation of polity also empowered the marginalized communities and enabled them to synchronize their aspirations with the upwardly mobile middle classes. As a corollary to the ongoing process of economic reforms, the trajectory of urbanization registered an upward swing. At present, one out of every three Indians is an urbanite. The middle class has virtually exploded in numbers from 25 million in 1996 to 160 million currently and if the current trend continues, it may be around 300 million by the end of 2020. This makes it a sizable chunk of our electorate which any political party can ignore at its own peril. Out of 543 Lok Sabha constituencies, 200 fall in the urban zones where the role of the urban middle class will be crucial in deciding the electoral fortunes of the candidates. The rapid strides made in Information Communication technologies (ICT) have also facilitated the emergence of middle class as a potent force in democratic India. Their protests do not require leaders or grand organizers to gain visibility as mutual exchange of ideas can be done by the mere click of a mouse. Social media, internet and face book have provided the platform for the middle class to engage with each other on matters that concern them and hence a seemingly, innocuous issue can snowball into a major issue. The middle class upsurge has caught the administration on the wrong foot on several occasions due to its unpredictability or the phenomenon of flash mobs.

It is not the case of India only but some regime changes that have taken place in Africa and the Arab world have been brought about by the grand net connectivity between the disenchanted working class and the unemployed youth hit hard by economic recession. The Occupy Wall Street Movement in USA was the outcome of the frustration of the working class/ middle class against the neo liberal economic order. Though the movement could not carry forward the momentum and soon petered out, the message that it wanted to convey reached all. Several governments in Europe like Spain, Greece, and Italy etc. had to go for austerity drive to tide over their increasing deficits compelling people to come out on the streets and shout slogans against neo capitalism. Today, the phenomenon that one is witnessing is the grand arrival of the global middle class connected from USA to Brazil to India to the Euro zone. The agenda is not only to ask for cushion against globalization shocks but political connotations are also there as we saw during the rise of Arab Spring. However, the problem with this class is that it lacks structures that can make the transformation, especially in polity, durable. The upsurge in Egypt was led by the educated, internet savvy youth and the working class but when elections took place, the fundamentalist Muslim Brotherhood and its allies captured power defeating the moderates who were more instrumental for the cause of the uprising. This happened because the educated moderate middle class was not organized and lacked structures to take on the might of the fundamentalists electorally. The Great Indian Middle Class Awakening has been brought about by better connectivity with the global developments and the homogenizing globalization syndrome. Till now, the electoral clout of this class may have been suspect but the 2013 Assembly Elections in Delhi proved beyond doubt the enormous strides made by the middle class movement politically. The Aam Aadmi Party, born out of the womb of the middle class upsurge, surprised the political pundits by bagging 28 out of 70 assembly seats and becoming the second largest party after BJP, relegating the Congress to the third position in the process. The AAP maintained equidistance from both the mainstream parties and canvassed for support on secular issues like governance & corruption unlike most of the parties who bank upon narrow identities and caste calculus to win seats. Don't be surprised if the Aam Aadmi Party forms the government in Delhi in the near future. When it comes to opinion making, the middle class is the most articulate among all the sections of our population and even the media is dominated by this class. In this age of information revolution, access to information is the most potent tool of empowerment. In this age of 24x7 channels, public opinion is shaped by the media, both electronic and print. Better connectivity and galloping urbanization have resulted in the proliferation of rural-urban fringe zones and today, even the rural areas are not untouched by the national mood/happenings. Rural India has undergone attitudinal transformation and it is not surprising that the middle class sentiments are having a trickledown effect in the villages. The rules of the political games are changing and in the coming years, urban middle class may become the most sought after constituency. Increased interflows of people between urban and rural areas have led to greater interactions between them and today, the rural flocks have developed a line of thinking similar to the urbanites as far as national issues are concerned. The gigantic strides made by ICT and the penetration of cable televisions in the rural homes have made the commoners aware of the national political trajectory.

The new middle class has no qualms against taking on the might of the state because it is not the product of Nehruvian socialism and its fate is not tied to state employment and pensions. Politics of patronage, symbolism and handing dole outs to them is not going to work as the aspirations of middle class has gone up a notch higher. Our much hyped democracy has failed to provide answers to the various ills that are plaguing our system with the political class evading responsibility and accountability. The trust deficit between the ruling class and the middle class has widened. Politics based on narrow identity markers like caste, language; ethnicity and religion have torn the social fabric of the nation apart and holding back its forward march. Armed with better education and information, the middle class can easily see through the nefarious designs of our vote bank obsessed political class. Nepotism, kinship, preferential treatment to favoured groups, bazaar canteen model of economy and feudality that characterize our economy are simply not compatible with the free ethos of the market economy. Naturally the middle class is feeling exasperated and the feeling that nothing could be achieved by being merely a passive onlooker has gained momentum. The middle class comprises of a substantial youth population who are not entrenched in past, tend to look ahead and desire active participation with the state on matters that concern them. The surfacing of a strong civil society, the pro active role of the media and the recrudescence of judicial activism has led to the gradual expansion of basic fundamental rights with innovative judicial interpretations. The coming into effect of RTI, the Citizen's Charter, e governance etc. has had far reaching repercussions and these initiatives have not reached the public on a platter but the civil society, propelled by the educated middle classes, struggled for them. Public interest litigations calling for more accountability on the part of the political class, electoral reforms to purge the system from the criminal elements and measures to bring administration closer to the people are steps that were taken by a reluctant political class due to intense pressure from this articulate class. Strong anti rape law and fast tracking of rape cases trials were enacted by the political executive in the wake of a lot of hue and cry made by the urban middle classes on the roads of the national capital and other major cities. Now, politicians are gradually realizing that they can no longer ignore the middle class and their electoral fortunes are not confined to rural India only. Moreover, this class has emerged as a nuisance for the politicians as they are better informed, conscious of their rights and cannot be taken for a ride.

The dalit activists and the mandalites may blame the middle class upsurge as being largely by the upper castes but the hard fact is that this class has in it a considerable sprinkling of the upward mobile sections of the dalits and the backwards who have taken advantage of the positive affirmative programmes of the state and climbed up the social economic developmental ladder. They have benefitted immensely from the new economic reforms and though they may be having reservations about some aspects of LPG, overall they are in agreement with the unfolding of reforms. The middle class shares the same aspirations, the same vision and the same interests and is not faction ridden on account of caste or other identity markers. The growing strength of the movement threatens the caste obsessed dalit movement as today, the young well off dalits are more likely to go with the opinion of the middle class than with their own sectarian movement. In a country where 65 percent of the population is less than 35 years of age, the younger, better educated dalits have less inclination to ideological moorings and are not too impressed with the dalit politics of symbolism and patronage. The growing numbers of these young middle class dalits are already giving sleepless nights to the protagonists of the dalit movement. These dalits do not want to lead a segregated life and are rather more interested in swimming along with the national mainstream. With the increase in the level of socio economic development, there is a possibility of more and more dalits, especially the youth swelling the middle class ranks having common interests with the upper castes and the backward castes. This may drive the last nails in the coffin of the dalit movement. The issues raised by the middle class are mostly secular and affect the day to day life of the common people. **The consolidation of this class as vote bank may sound a death knell to the politics of caste and religion and check the growth of undesirable sub altern movements that lack an all inclusive character. Hence the vehement opposition to the middle class surge in the anti corruption movement.**

Now, let us come to another point of criticism of the Anna crusade by the dalit leadership. The dalit movement wants reservation for the dalits in the proposed Lok Pal as it feels that in the absence of dalit representation, the dalit interests will be severely compromised. Just consider the absurdity and the hollowness of the demand. Reserving seats in the Lok Pal is not like reserving seats in public employment; it raises several pertinent and disturbing questions relating to the idea of governance and representation. Is not the dalit demand premised on the point that fair governance for people of any community can only be catered to by people belonging to the same community? Is it not a denigration of the highest institutions of the state and a question mark on the very notion of its impartiality? It lends credence to the argument that even the top most institutions of state cannot be counted upon to act independently of identity considerations. The dalit demand endorses its lack of trust in the state. If such divisive trends are not dealt with sternly but encouraged, a time may come when demands for reservation are made in institutions like the Supreme Court, the High Courts, the Election Commission, the Central Information Commission, the Central Vigilance Commission and the Union Public Service Commission or even in the cabinet/council of ministers. Tomorrow, the dalit activists may say that since the Indian Prime Minister is a non dalit, he cannot understand the problems relating to dalits and for proper justice to the dalits, a dalit PM must be installed. It may be a throwback to the early colonial days when British judges mandatorily presided over cases involving Europeans. The individual becomes important; his background becomes important and the assumption that decision making is more a variable of caste and background than the tenets of the constitution gains ground. The very foundation of the office of institution suffers because of the fact that when an individual holds any office, the belief is that the role played by him allows him to look beyond the identity of those affected by the decision. After all the distinction between reserving seats in the government with that of the Lok Pal is that, in the former efforts are made to give a say to all the stake holders and ensure that their concerns are adequately represented before arrival of the final decision. The final result is contingent on the merits of the case. At some point, only merit matters; logic matters more than the identity or background of the person making the argument. If not we may well move to a situation when backward caste judges will make decisions on cases involving OBCs? Dalit judges will preside over cases dealing with dalits. And just think what would happen if macro identity gets discarded in favour of micro identities? The nation could, in the name of fostering inclusiveness, be taking a long walk back into past, freezing the social architecture in the present form.

Mandalisation of polity and dalit movement

The mandalisation of polity in the early nineties following the reservation of 27 percent vacancies in government jobs for the Other Backward Castes (OBC) led to gigantic transformation in polity. The reservation for backward castes was later extended to the hubs of higher education and the universities/ colleges. The OBCs constitute about 40-50 percent of our population and traditionally; they possessed rural land assets plus political power. They never faced caste related discriminations like that of the dalits. They have always been an integral part of Hinduism and its social system fold and unlike dalits had frequent interactions and social intercourse with the upper castes. They accepted the Hindu rituals and never showed offence towards sacred Hindu scriptures, the Vedas or the Gita. They never rejected the Rams and the Krishnas and there are occasions when they lay claim over Krishna and do not hesitate to retell the story. The backwards form a wide socio political and developmental continuum, with the lower end of the chain displaying identical traits with the dalits and the upper end resembling the developmental parameters of the upper castes. Economically, a fair percentage of the backward communities like the Kurmis in Bihar, the Yadavs and the Jats in UP, the Lingayats and the Vokkalingas in Karnataka and the Reddys in Andhra are at par or even higher than the upper castes. The creamy layer of the backward castes has been kept out of the purview of reservation.

Unprecedented political mobilization and polarization, in the wake of the Mandal wave, on caste lines saw the surfacing of a powerful backward leadership at the helm of affairs in the politically important states of Bihar and UP. Strong backward caste leaders like Mulayam Singh, Lallu Yadav, Nitish Kumar and Sharad Yadav jostled for power in the Hindi heartland. The dalit movement extended its support to the backward caste leadership and supported the implementation of Mandal Commission report. Kanshiram began to give shape to his astute political vision of bringing the dalits and the backwards on a common platform with his concept of Bahujan. Ram Vilas Paswan, another firebrand dalit leader from Bihar, backed Lallu Yadav in government formation in the early nineties. The dalit movement intended to create solidarity between the backwards and the dalits, thus bringing to the fore a powerful political grouping that had the potential to keep the upper castes, the so called Manuwadi forces out of power. But has this political prognosis of Kanshiram gained acceptance? Have the forces of Mandalisation and Dalitisation managed to forge any unity of purpose?

Let us examine the ground realities between the backwards and the dalits as prevalent in different parts of the country. Politically resurgent backwards gained access to land assets in rural India. From a historical perspective also, the powerful sections of the backward castes had traditional possessions of land. The upper castes headed towards the urban corridors as they were convinced that it was not their government and they were reconciled to their minority status as electorate in most of India—for them, liberalization and privatization offered hope. The landed backward castes became the masters and employed the landless dalits to work on their farmlands. Master-servant relationship between the two got institutionalized in the process. The attitude of this backward landed class is no better than the attitude of the upper castes towards the dalits. There are various instances when it is found that the backwards avoid intermingling with the dalits at the social occasions, refuse to accept food/water from them and bear the same prejudices towards them as upper castes. Ground level hostilities have occasionally flared up between the Yadavs and the dalits in UP and the paswans vs yadavs in Bihar. Western UP is such a place where jats and dalits have never co-existed peacefully. In the southern state of Tamil Nadu, dalits and the backward Vanniyars have upped the ante against each other.

The brute numerical preponderance of the OBCs, their fragmentation into various castes and sub castes and the huge prospects of mobilization/consolidation led to a clamour among politicians to outdo each other in pandering to the OBCs. With the constitutional sanction to pamper in the form of reservation to the backwards, appeasement of the non dalits and the non Brahmins became a political reality. The bigger national parties like the Congress and the BJP that were traditionally dominated by upper caste leadership saw a change in their social demographic profile as more and more OBC leaders rose in the party ranks. In a predominantly bania—Brahmin leadership dominated party like the BJP, the mascots of Hindutva turned out to be backward caste leaders like Kalyan Singh, Uma Bharti, Vinay katiyaar and Narendra Modi. Even the powerful Yeddurappa, deep down into the south in Karnataka is a Lingayat, a strong OBC community. This, indeed, is surprising. This manifests the extent to which the political parties have to go to woo the backward caste communities.

Now a few developments in the realm of Indian polity give us glimpses into the likely trajectory of relationship between the dalits and the OBCs. Come 2007 Assembly Elections in Uttar Pradesh. Mayawati is crowned as the Queen of UP and what does she do? The dalit tsarina goes on a rapid and indiscriminate construction spree in Noida, Lucknow and other parts of the state. The Dalit Prerna Sthal comes up at Noida at huge state expenditure, followed by the construction of Ambedkar parks, statues of the BSP symbol elephants and idols of the icons of dalit polity like Ambedkar, Phule, Periyar, Kanshiram and Mayawati, herself. Her efforts at blatant display of dalit assertiveness do not end here. She embarks on a name changing spree of the districts—the names of Hathras, Kanpur Dehat, Amethi and Amroha are changed to Mahamaya Nagar, Ramabai Nagar, Chattrapati Sahu Maharaj Nagar and Jyoti Ba Phule Nagar respectively. She does her nomenclature based on the names of the dalit icons and in doing so; she does not even spare the constituencies, nurtured by the Gandhi family. All the welfare and developmental programmes of the state are named after the dalit icons. Official postings and transfers are done on caste lines. Cases registered under SC/ST act witness an increase.

Come 2012 Assembly Elections in UP. BSP is decimated and gets a paltry 80 seats though the voting percentage difference between SP and BSP, the two rivals is a mere 3-4 percentage, making things amply clear for the celebrating Samajwadi supporters that Mayawati is far from being finished politically. The Akhilesh Singh led Samajwadi Party takes over the reins of power with an impressive landslide victory. Let's take a look at what the Samajwadi government is doing. The welfare schemes named after the dalit icons are scrapped and new ones emerge named after the socialist greats like Lohia, Karpoori Thakur and Jai Prakash Narayan. Construction of Janeshwar Mishra Park and a Centre for Studies on JP Narayan are proposed to be set up at Lucknow. Maintenance expenditure on Ambedkar parks and other dalit monuments is reduced and there is a talk of utilizing the vacant spaces of the park areas for holding community functions and opening of schools and hospitals. The order of the BSP Government changing the names of the districts stands cancelled. Criminal cases are lodged against the BSP functionaries and bureaucrats for alleged irregularities committed during the rule of the BSP government. Atrocities committed on the dalits witness a multifold increase. SC/ST cases registered against non dalits are withdrawn in several cases and the media is abuzz with reports of the houses/properties of dalits being vandalized by the backwards.

The policies of both the parties are aimed at consolidation of social categories and pitting them one against the other using governmental developmental schemes and acts of symbolism in the form of construction of statues of their respective icons.

Ambedkarism stands face to face with Lohia-ism in this Hindi speaking state. Lohia, regarded as the brain behind OBC consolidation in the north that ultimately led to the mandalisation of polity was reborn. The OBC leadership of the state commands unflinching support of their caste groups and are attached to the ground realities though the national secular perspective is missing. **There is no denying the fact that mandalisation resulted in the real empowerment of the backward castes and communities and led to their increased visibility but simultaneously, it has engendered blatant casteism and that too, in the garb of social justice.** The principles underlying the socialist movement and the ideology of the socialist stalwarts of our polity like Karpoori Thakur, Lohia, JP Narayan and Narendra Dev have been discarded by the present day OBC leadership though publically, it professes to carry forward the legacy of the socialist greats. After attaining power, the backward leadership has turned politics into some sort of family business and apart from talking about caste mobilization; they have nothing concrete to offer to Indian polity. Unlike Ambedkar's reservation for dalits which was meant to remove the age old untouchability, caste based discriminations and the deplorable socio economic conditions of the dalits, the implementation of the Mandal Commission Report has acted as a sort of political resource for the OBC leadership which sees caste identity as an asset to be utilised politically in the path to the attainment of political power. No change in the direction of UP politics seems possible and this battle of dalits and backwards will continue, with fortunes oscillating according to the political tides. Massive state funds will continue to be splurged on the names of Lohia and Ambedkar while the state of Uttar Pradesh will continue to languish at the bottom in terms of national human development indicators. Corruption and development issues will be relegated to the periphery and the elections will be fought on realignment and forging of strong caste and community linkages.

Let's turn our attention to the southern part of Indian peninsula and see how the relationship has evolved between the dalits and the OBCs. The Dravidian movement is basically associated with social egalitarianism and struggle against caste, gender and linguistic inequalities. However, recently Uthapuram came into spotlight on account of caste wall that was erected to segregate the scheduled caste population from the dominant backward caste communities. A state level party in Tamil Nadu having around 7-8 percent vote share, PMK does not hide the fact that it stands for the interests of the backward caste Vanniyars and that it is avowedly anti dalit. In view of the coming elections, the party has reportedly intensified its anti dalit pitch by evoking paranoia and insecurity among the backwards. Dalit youths are being targeted for alluring the Vanniyar girls into marrying them. There are calls for the scrapping of SC/ST act on the ground that they are being misused by the dalit politicians to settle political scores with the non dalits. Large scale violence against dalits was carried out by the PMK workers at Dharmapuri and Marakkanam in the state. However, it comes as a welcome relief that the major Dravidian parties, the DMK and the AIDMK have completely supported the dalits and the VCK (Viduthalai Chiruthaigal Katchi), the dalit party that is antagonistic to the PMK. PMK was politically isolated and some of its leaders were incarcerated. The meeting between Ramadoss and Akhilesh Yadav raises some eyebrows whether the backward politics of the cow belt and the southern peninsula are contemplating to find a common ground.

It is indeed unthinkable that such practices of untouchability still persist and that too in the socially progressive state of Tamil Nadu. No doubt, Dravidianism has created social inclusiveness in the state and helped to check the spread of communalism but at the same time; it cannot be denied that the Dravidian parties have refused to engage in full scale land reforms or other structural programmes to rein in the caste inequalities thus showing their true casteist face. More than hundred years have elapsed since the dawn of social reform movement but even today one would struggle to find dalits who have made it to the top in Tamil polity though the dalits comprise about 18 percent of the total state population.Caste based movements and parties like the Vanniyar Sangam have witnessed quite a few mobilisations to expose and confront the dominant caste basis of the Dravidian parties who derive their main support base from the OBCs. The dalits may have participated in the movement but their role has never been recognised and they have been treated as mere vote banks to be assuaged during the time of hustings. Populist measures for the downtrodden like distribution of TV sets and cheap rice are mainly directed at public consumption to prove the love of Dravidian parties for the dalits and that too, in the glare of the media. It would not be out of context to mention that the landed OBCs/farmers in the state get a lot of subsidies like cheap electricity but this does not make headlines. When MNREGA threatened to reduce supply of cheap labour for these land owning castes, they became aggressive and formed caste associations to put down the challenges posed by the landless/marginal farmers most of who were dalits. Many regions of the state witnessed clashes between the dalits and the backwards, with dalits often being at the receiving end. The Dravidian parties have been successful in camouflaging the caste basis of social structures; the dalits have failed to understand the empty rhetoric, symbolism and populism of these parties and have been taken for a ride on numerous occasions. The dalit voters had drifted away from the Congress in the hope of getting a better deal from the Dravidian parties but their hopes have been dashed. Very soon, they realised they were mere vote banks and hence can't get a share in power even though the mainstream Tamil parties continued to talk of social revolution and contemplate to add a touch of social radicalism in their programmes like Mid Day Meals. The schemes meant for the Adi Davidars have never really taken off, the anti caste message has never been taken to the masses in a big way and the subaltern voices have been trampled upon in the party organisations. The fast few years have seen rising animosities between the dalits and the backwards, with a clamour growing among the backwards for the repeal of SC/ST Act.

The years after 1980s were a watershed in the annals of Tamil polity as the dalits became disenchanted with the regional outfits and began to organise/ mobilise themselves for taking on the hegemony of the

Dravidian parties. Parties like the VCK and the Dalit panthers sprung up, started agitations for the dalit cause and soon there was a new voice of the subalterns. They became vocal in their demands for a separate dalit identity and a space in Tamil polity. Slogans like "Our Votes for Ourselves" rent the air and dalit parties threatened to attract the dalit voters towards them away from the mainstream Dravidian parties. The downtrodden were aghast at the treatment meted out to them and were determined to teach a lesson or two to the Dravidian parties. The socio political atmosphere vitiated, the dalits refused to perform the traditional tasks assigned to them in the countrysides, confronted the caste discriminations head on, organised themselves into caste associations and raised demands for implementation of land reforms to benefit them. The Dalit Panthers took to the streets to press for the dalit demands and soon, a series of caste clashes started between the dalits and the dominant OBCs. The backwards retaliated and were not hesitant to heap caste atrocities on the dalits.

Various studies have shown that the OBC upsurge in Tamil polity was more non Brahmin than anti Brahmin. The Dravidian parties snatched power from the dominance of the brahminical minority and broke their socio political monopoly. They also made use of their immense clout to stall the ambitious land reforms and social schemes meant for the dalits. The fractured nature of caste dominance in the state where no sub group is politically, socially or numerically dominant has blurred the extent to which social power and political power are intertwined. The Thevars, Grounders, Naickars, Vadars and Vanniyars are being aggressively courted by the Dravidian parties. Unlike UP, there are only two major political parties in the state and hence votes tend to split up in two directions. A very high percentage of votes are required for victory in any constituency thus making things amply clear for the dalits that they can't stand on their own and must look out for support of other caste groupings or any major Dravidian party. Most of these dalit parties lack deep financial pockets making things difficult for them when contesting elections. The decline of the Congress in Tamil Nadu has reduced their options and it is not surprising to see them taking up the cause of Tamil Elam in their quest for separate Tamil identity and pride.

The dalit movement has to prepare itself against the challenges thrown at it by the rising forces of mandalism. It may have lambasted the forces of Manuwad for decades but now, it seems that the OBCs are threatening their political territory. The proposed constitutional amendment bill to facilitate reservation for dalits in promotion for government jobs has already run into rough weather due to protests from the Samajwadi Party, a party supposedly of backward castes. DMK is also not happy with the decision of the union government to bring this bill to the Parliament. The irony is that their opposition is not based on the violation of the constitutional provision of 'Equality of Opportunity' but the fact that this provision is applicable only to dalits and not OBCs. The stringent stand taken by Samajwadi Party against reservation in promotions is due to the prevailing ground realities in the state of UP. The SP knows all too well that even if it supports the bill, the dalits are not going to vote for it. The passage of the bill is only going to increase the importance of the dalit leader Mayawati and consolidate her sway over the dalit constituency. Unlike the traditionally upper caste dominated parties like the Congress, BJP and even the communist parties who prefer to remain tightlipped on sensitive dalit issues, the OBC dominated parties have no qualms in taking the dalit activists/leadership head on. Unlike the upper caste parties, these mandalite outfits are not driven by self guilt or a messianic zeal to reform the social set up but purely by the political interest of consolidating their vote banks. For them, real politick is the driving mantra rather than social activism for the dalit cause. There is every possibility of this bill going the Women's Reservation Bill way, which coincidentally is also facing the fury of the mandalites and is yet to see the light of the day. The OBC dominated parties are demanding a sub reservation clause in the bill for the OBC women within the overall prescribed ceiling for the women.

The dalit leadership has never been comfortable with the Congress since pre and post independence days and now, the unfolding of the dalit—OBC acrimonious relationship point to certain developments whose historical perspective needs to be examined. The record of Indian politics after or even before independence shows that the socialist leaders were tied umbilically with the Congress. Though Congress leadership comprised highly educated, upper caste people, landlords and princes most of who had nothing to do social revolution, it has to be accepted that within the party, there was a dedicated cadre of social activists who took up burning issues relating to the masses. Though they may have belonged to the upper strata of the society, they took it as a badge of honour to represent the cases of the deprived people. Despite being a part of the upholders of status quo, they always found ways to reach out to the downtrodden and champion their cause. It was Nehru who blessed JP Narayan to form the Congress Socialist Party in 1934 with the mandate to work for the creation of an egalitarian social order within the fold of the Congress. There was a tussle within the party between the conservatives and the socialists like JP Narayan, Lohia, Narendra Dev and Ashok Mehta. The conservatives wanted status quo while the socialists were in favour of ushering in measures that would lead to far reaching social repercussions like land reforms, abolition of privy purses and nationalization of banks. Ultimately, in the face of the obdurate stand of the Congress towards their demands, they parted ways with their parent party. It is interesting to observe that the later Congress governments, both at the centre and the states were not averse to acceding to demands of the socialists like abolition of privy purses, nationalization of banks and going in for land reforms. When the power struggle within the Congress intensified in the late sixties, Indira Gandhi turned towards left and enacted a slew of socialist measures to silence the old guards of the party, commonly referred to as Syndicates.

Charan Singh was a Jat leader from western Uttar Pradesh. Though the jats were traditionally prosperous agricultural communities, Charan Singh considered himself to be the leader of the backward communities, farmers and peasants. Despite being a part of the Congress in the early part of his political career, he was not comfortable with the fact of the upper caste dominance of the party apparatus and addressed several meetings of the farmers and the backwards to make them aware of their political rights. He felt that the upper castes dominated polity and bureaucracy while the dalits got benefits of state reservation, leaving the OBCs in the lurch. Ultimately, he left the Congress party to form his own party i.e. the Lok Dal. He, along with Devi Lal of Haryana and Karpoori Thakur of Bihar, formed an axis of backward assertion in the Hindi belt. Many political observers have asserted that it was Charan Singh who orchestrated the plot to deny the towering dalit leader, Jagjivan Ram a shot at Prime Ministership reflecting his anti dalit feelings. **There is no gainsaying the fact that for most of the socialists, the dalit agenda was not the driving factor; rather they were more interested in espousing the cause of the farming communities, most of whom were backwards. The common ground between the dalits and the OBCs was never there for reconciliation as their socio economic interests were mutually contradictory.**

Land reforms, green revolution and community development extension programmes increased the prosperity and political clout of the OBCs which got reinforced after the Mandalisation of our polity. The current lot of mandalite leadership in our country like Lalu Yadav, Mulayam Singh, Sharad Yadav and Nitish Kumar inherited the political legacy of the above mentioned socialist leaders. Most of them cut their political teeth under the tutelage of the Lohias and the Charan Singhs and the Karpoori Thakurs. For them, the dalits were simply vote banks and not partners in power sharing or governance. They may have opposed the Congress but had a tinge of Congressism in their genetic makeup.

The contours of the evolving dalit—OBC relationship have given rise to certain pertinent questions that should agitate the minds of dalit thinkers. Should the dalit movement oppose the OBC leadership ideologically and enter into a confrontation with them? Should they move towards the upper castes to counter the mandalites or should they contemplate to find a common ground with them on the plank of social justice?

Communism: Why at odds with the dalit movement

One of the puzzles affecting Indian polity, that still remains largely unresolved, is the trust deficit between the dalit movement and the communists. Both the strands draw sustenance from the same broad social groupings like the peasants, the factory workers and the landless labourers. Ambedkar was not a great admirer of Marx but believed in the socialism of the Fabian kind. He was not convinced with Marx's concept of class war/ revolution on the part of the proletariat to defeat the bourgeoisie and the forces of capitalism. He was not sure whether capture of power by the proletariat would not lead to dictatorship. Class may have its relevance in the western industrialized countries where the social composition of working class is not much diverse. But, conditions in India do differ drastically. Most of the organizations or unions of working class formed here are divided on caste, community or religious lines and workers/members of these bodies owe more allegiance to their identity markers than the organization. Many government departments have ST/ST cells within them for dalit related issues. So apart from class or occupational solidarity, caste solidarity cannot be ruled out. For Ambedkar, caste was a social reality in India that could not be swept under the carpet. For him, caste was the prime driving force that manifested itself into acute levels of deprivation and inequalities between different sections of the population.

For the communists, all the problems faced by the society have their genesis in class conflicts or class differences. They kept themselves above caste as they had the firm conviction that class cannot be defined on the basis of caste. Caste considerations were a taboo for them as they felt that caste operates as an obstacle in the forging of class solidarity. The left originated in the 20th century and since its inception, it has left no stone unturned in its agenda of discrediting and alienating the dalit movement. The solidarity between the peasants, working class and the landless rural workers has not yet been achieved due to the interplay of caste and class factors. The engagement between the left and the dalits has been marked by cynicism because the left feels that the identity driven dalit politics has added sectarianism, much to the chagrin of the non dalits and led it away from the material problems of the underprivileged people. The communists have also adopted a reactionary posture towards the dalit leadership which they feel, is driving a wedge between the masses by seeing everything through the prism of caste. They are fully convinced that the dalits do not want the doing away of caste but want concessions within the existing structure of caste. The economic perspective which distinguishes the communists from other mainstream parties is something which seems to be lacking in the dalit movement.

Now, let us come to the other side of the picture. The communists are berated by the dalits for virtually making no contribution to the dismantling of feudal social structures and living under the grand illusion that once class solidarity, read proletariat solidarity is achieved, questions like feudalism in rural India and the institution of caste would become redundant. The dalit intellectuals are also suspicious of the fact that the top political leadership of the major communist parties, even today, is dominated by the upper castes.

Whatever directions the two movements take, one thing is crystal clear. The lack of cohesion and congruence between them does not augur well for the materialization of the social revolution in India. Based on their objectives, both the streams were supposed to be natural allies, a thing that failed to happen.

The Indian polity has been plagued by the caste factor right from the days of the colonial rule. The imperial forces exploited the division of Indian society based on caste/community/religious lines in order to buttress the foundations of the British Empire and pit one set of Indians against the other. Post independence, the Nehruvian line of thinking supported the setting up of heavy industries—the so called temples of modern society. It was presumed that the ongoing forces of industrialization and the concomitant urbanization would lead to the gradual withering of the institution of caste and lay the foundations of an inclusive and secular society. The land reforms were sought to be undertaken urgently to prepare the ground for an agrarian social revolution as it was felt that until and unless, the social dominance of the landed class was not ruptured in favour of the majority landless marginalized class, a more equal and egalitarian society would not develop. Moreover, the question of caste was intricately linked with land and hence, for weakening caste it was necessary to resolve the land imbroglio. However, just the opposite happened. The feudal/semi feudal elements most of whom belonged to the upper and intermediate backward castes, had powerful connections with the ruling parties and so, apart from half baked measures, nothing substantial could come out of land reforms. States like Bihar and UP failed in ushering in social revolution and that is one of the reasons why the caste factor has got embedded so deeply in the social fabric of both these states. In Bihar/Jharkhand, the rise of the left wing extremism led to bloody clashes between the naxal sympathizers/lower caste landless and the upper caste/ intermediate caste landowners. What's remarkable is the fact that many massacres of the dalits took place when the backwards/mandalites were ensconced in the seat of power at Patna. Not only this, it is widely believed that the backward leadership of the state kept silent deliberately when the private armies of the landlords tried to decimate the voices of the poor, hapless dalits. Here, more than the caste factor, it was the coming into interplay of the combined interest of both the upper and powerful OBC castes that led to the perpetration of atrocities on the lower castes. Take the case of West Bengal. When the communists took over the reins of power from the Congress in the mid seventies, the naxal menace was sought to be contained through the meaningful implementation of land reforms. The change of social dynamics in rural Bengal prevented bloodbath and a possible fragmentation of polity on caste lines. Even today when you compare west Bengal with a Bihar or a UP, the first thing that strikes you is the fact that the level of political mobilization of the lower castes is much less in Bengal. There is nothing like a backward or a dalit caste party there.

The dalit leaders starting from Phule to Ambedkar were steadfast in opposing caste discrimination and calling for an end to brahminical hegemony. They attacked the ancient and the feudal structures but refused to go deep into the underlying reasons for the perpetuation of feudalism. **The dalit leadership failed to organize peasantry for a total agrarian revolution as its obsession with caste prevented it from examining the agrarian relationship between the landlords, tenants and the landless labourers and the accompanying societal equations. It kept itself preoccupied with superficial demands like reservation and representation that catered to the interests of dalit elites and refused to look into the plight of their fellow brethren in rural areas who constituted the overwhelming majority.**

The demands of electoral polity and the coming into effect of universal adult suffrage led to rapid political mobilization of people on caste lines. The dalit assertion was followed by the assertion/empowerment of backward castes in the post Mandal era. Caste is a social reality in our polity. In India, the concept of society/kinship emerged first and then, the concept of state came into vogue. So, it is not surprising that Indians owe more allegiance to the society/kinship/ community, in comparison to the state. The decision of the Government of India to call for caste census of backward castes is the first of its kind in independent India and is certainly a regressive step. Let us not forget that many leaders of the ruling party were not initially in favour of the caste census but ultimately, the backward leadership of all the major political parties compelled the Union government to do so. Women's reservation Bill has not yet become a reality in our country just because the backward caste politicians of our country do not want it. Take the recent phenomenon of caste rallies. The caste rallies came into limelight in the 1980s with BSP making extensive use of such rallies to mobilize their supporters. Since then, caste rallies have been organized by all the parties, including Congress though the facts remain that the regional parties are more adept in the art of caste mobilization. **Such rallies are mere euphemisms for caste solidarity because the harsh reality is that such rallies are platforms to engage in vitriolic attacks on rival communities.** The Allahabad High Court has recently banned the holding of such rallies. Though the judgement appears to be debatable, the real intention behind the verdict is certainly not wrong.

It is not only the left that has not been able to come out of the caste-class conundrum, the right Hindutva forces also seem to be discovering the spectra of caste. The growth of Hindutva in Karnataka has been synonymous with the rise of Lingayats, a powerful backward community in Karnataka. The BJP captured power in Karnataka, not because of any Hindutva wave but because of the support and political mobilization of the Lingayat community, spearheaded by the powerful Lingayat leader, Yeddurappa. The myth of the Hindutva Karnataka was exploded when BJP failed to come to power on its own, after expelling Yeddurappa. Hindutva BJP had to capitulate before the bargaining power/ electoral clout of the Lingayats.

So, should we assume that caste is destined to stay in India? Is the dalit movement right in repudiating the over reliance of the communists on the class theory?

Communists point out the divisions between labour and capital but remain mum when confronted with the fact that there are divisions within labour as well. In India, all the labour unions and the employee unions are divided on caste lines and they are affiliated to political parties who champion the cause of certain castes. Naturally, caste aspirations are never lost sight of. Let us take another example from rural India. Most of the landless labour class who works on the fields belongs to the lower dalit castes while the land owning class comprises of the upper castes and the powerful socially dominant backward classes. Hence the level of backwardness and the possession of land get inadvertently linked to caste. The communists may see this phenomenon in terms of class—land owning class and land deprived class. However, in the realm of class, caste can't be wished away. In India, generally upper class has been associated with upper castes and the lower class with the backwards and the dalits. In the initial years after independence, this class-caste association was right to a great extent but to extend this association to present times is a bit fallacious. Unlike caste which is static, class is porous and has constantly evolving boundaries. State affirmative programmes, political empowerment of dalits/backwards and the mannerisms of our patronage democracy have made sure that caste and class always never go hand in hand. A good number of upper caste populations can't lay claim to upper class tag today as vote bank politics has led to reduction in their economic clout. Many backwards and dalits have improved their socio economic status, have become upwardly mobile and may, rightly, be bracketed in the upper class club. The middle class upsurge that the nation is witnessing today is not about only the upper castes but there is a fair sprinkling in it of dalits and the backwards. These people talk of class deprivation and not caste deprivation. Educated, articulate and connected with global developments, this class is not blinded by the narrowness of its agenda and often, speaks the language of universalism. It aligns its cause with the people on a global scale and abides by the dictum—act locally, think globally. It is in solidarity with the global people right from the Euro Zone to the USA and tends to think on class lines, rather than caste lines. The rise of the middle class has the potential to disrupt the game plan of the parties which have made effective use of the caste plank and based their polity on narrow, short term gains rather than the real empowerment of the communities by investing in their HRD. The politics of patronage and symbolism displayed by these parties have no meaning for the educated within the community whose aspirations have gone up in the wake of the globalization wave. The political class may try to derive consolation from the fact that their electoral fortunes are tied with the rural power that are in majority and not the urban middle class but then, history testifies that most of the changes being brought about in the world were spearheaded by the working middle class. The Arab Spring which brought changes in Tunisia, Libya and Egypt was essentially a secular uprising comprising techno savvy middle class youth who worked in impressive coordination with the working class and the trade unions. Working class unrest in Italy, Greece, France, USA and England was nothing but manifestation of working class and unemployed youth frustration with the pro capital governments.

The latest countries to face civilian unrest are Turkey and Brazil with reasons varying from corruption to anti people policies. In a nutshell, the phenomenon we are witnessing is the congruence of interests of the global middle class/working class who are getting increasingly frustrated and exasperated with their national governments. The feeling of disdain towards the political class and the lack of confidence in the political culture of today are something that characterize the middle class and this certainly is not good news for the politicians. The new economic reforms and the penetration of internet, mobile phones and information communication technologies have brought about a global connect.

In India too, vast socio economic inequality exists and the society has been bifurcated into have and have nots. The billionaires, supposed to be the second largest in number in the world, co-existing amidst the vast sea of ignorant and desperate masses. The sky rocketing apartments housing luxurious flats co-exist with the despair and hopelessness of stenching slums at their feet. The plying together of the BMWs and the bullock carts on the same road is a common sight. With the approach of the global uncertainty, the common people are feeling the pinch in the aftermath of reduction in their purchasing ability due to high levels of inflation. The youth are finding it difficult to find employment venues. The obsession of state with fiscal deficit has led to cuts in pro poor subsidies, welfare expenditure and expenditure in education and health sectors resulting in increased deprivation levels among the poor and the lower middle class. The same state has no qualms in providing tax concessions and fiscal incentives to the corporate class to the tune of 5 lakh crores.

The dalit or the backward caste politicians/ bureaucrats/industrialists tend to identify themselves more with the class interests of the elites and in course of time copy their attitudes and mannerisms. The working class, the common masses, the daily wage workers working on agricultural farmlands or in brick kilns or at construction sites etc. face the same economic hardships and the same humiliation at the hands of their employers who do not discriminate a dalit from a non dalit. Castes may be different but the problems associated with their occupations/class remain the same. Dalit leadership/activists tend to give the impression as if castes matter more and problems are there because of their caste. **No doubt, caste determines class in the Indian context to a great extent but this phenomenon is under attack today. Social set up is changing, the patriarchal society is shrinking in space and communists in India are yet not ready to give precedence to caste over class.**

Now, let us come to the issue of urbanization. It is true that caste factor cannot be completely ruled out from urban life. The urban morphology reveals it. If you go to the slums, makeshift dwelling arrangements below a bridge or near railway stations and other impoverished urban zones, the first thing that strikes you is the fact that majority population of this area comprises the lower castes. In better living areas, the landlords won't give you rented accommodation without ascertaining your caste. The urban occupational structure reveals that most of the dalits are engaged in low menial jobs of the informal sector, eateries and construction sites. However, despite this the urban environment provides the dalits freedom from the oppressed stratified rural society. Common public restaurants, common public transport, common public parks and the common government housing colonies facilitate the increasing social intercourse between the dalits and the non dalits. Caste dictated occupational structure is undergoing transformation with manual undignified jobs of cleaning and wiping being taken over by automated systems. Though it may take time but the urban life has the potential to create commonality of dalit and non dalit interests and ensure the gradual diminishing of caste importance.

Coming back to the caste-class paradox, it can't be denied that in contemporary Indian society, caste is a fact of life as our society is in transitional stage, having moved away from the primitive stage. It is yet to take birth into a modern industrial society. In a primitive society, caste and communities tend to subvert the public institutions that are not well developed. With the development of society, the importance of identity parameters decreases and there is a chorous for inclusiveness and universality of norms. The rise of middle class, the rules of neo liberalization and globalized world order and the deepening urbanization process are developments that enhance the class consciousness. In the coming days, caste consciousness may witness a decline, if not disappear from national consciousness. The incentives of caste may also see a decline.

Dalit movement—Hindutva and Buddhism

Post 1990, Hindutva has been a much debated topic within the country. Ramjanam Bhoomi movement starting with the silanayas during Rajiv Gandhi government, growing frustration of the people with the pseudo secular/appeasement policy of the Congress, Advani's Rath Yatra and the razing of the Babri Masjid in 1992 were the main factors responsible for polarization of Hindu votes on religious lines. This helped the right wing BJP to carve out a distinctive space for itself in Indian polity. The rise of Hindutva has led to far reaching ramifications in our country with political parties being divided into so called secular and non secular camps. There is a tussle and competition between parties for scoring brownie points over the exaggerated secularism debate. Though various interpretations of secularism and Hindutva are there, confusion still persists. Now, what exactly is this Hindutva and what ideology does it subscribe to?

According to Golwalkar, natives of India share a common culture and believe in India's common culture, history and ancestry. He believed that India's diversity in terms of customs, traditions and ways of worship was its uniqueness and this diversity was not without the strong underlying cultural basis which was essentially native. He believed that the Hindu natives with all their diversity shared among other things—the same philosophy of life, the same values and aspirations which formed a strong cultural bond and the civilisational basis of a nation. The RSS, the fountain head of Hinduism, with its slogan—one nation, one language, one culture, one religion—operates through a plethora of frontal organizations like the VHP, the Bajrang Dal and the ABVP. For RSS, Hindutva is a cultural concept, not a religious or a political ideology and includes Sikhs, Buddhists and Jains. The cultural nationality of India is Hindu, encompassing all those who are born here and who have adopted Bharat as their homeland, including Muslims, Parsis and the Christians.

Whatever may be the definitions regarding Hindutva put forth by its proponents, the dalit leadership/intelligentsia has remained very suspicious of its ideology. It perceives Hindutva as the very epitome of a stratified, hierarchal, brahminical social system that is inherently in conflict with its goals. Ambedkar was opposed to Hindu nationalists as RSS was dominated by upper caste leadership displaying brahminical orthodox leanings and its grand illusions of a united culturally and homogenous Bharat was an anathema to the exclusionary, sectarian dalit agenda of Ambedkar. Ambedkar's protest against the Hindu religion, for its endorsement of caste discriminations against the lower castes, led to his call for a change in religion among his followers. For him, spiritual salvation lay in Buddhism which was an indigenous, home grown religion based on compassion and egalitarianism, having place for dignity of the dalits. His conversion to Buddhism in 1956 at Nagpur was aimed at exhorting his followers to free themselves from the shackles of Hinduism, by finding solace in Buddhism and accepting it. Even after the death of Ambedkar, many dalits have continued to embrace Buddhism in bits and pieces and for many dalit scholars, this is the manifestation of the dalit movement's propensity to assert its cultural moorings and impart to itself, a separate identity that is distinct from Hinduism.

Many dalit thinkers argue that the depressed classes did not lie in the Vedic Chaturvarna scheme of stratification—the Brahmins, the kshetriyas, the Vaisyas and the Shudras—and hence lay outside the pale of Hinduism. Moreover, along with the tribals dalits form a separate class of citizens having different customs and religious practices, having their own deities and village gods. They also contend that without having the right to read the religious texts of Hinduism, without having access to Hindu temples and public places and without any social intercourse with the caste Hindus, how can they regard themselves to be part of the Hindu fold? Even during the widely regarded golden period of Indian history i.e. during the era of the Guptas, the untouchable Chandals were not allowed to enter the city gates within specified hours.

For the dalits, Buddha offers hope and the fact is that today in dalit weddings, it is not uncommon to see the figure of Buddha imprinted in place of Lord Ganesha in marriage invitation cards. Mayawati's creation of dalit monuments bear a touch of Buddhist architecture but to say that Buddhism, as a religion, has made its presence felt in India is a bit preposterous. The phenomenon of dalit conversions to Buddhism has not even led to a slight change in the religious demographic profile of the dalits. According to 2001 census,

Buddhists constitute less than 1 percent population of the country. As dalits constitute 16-18 percent population of the country, it can be safely assumed that more than 90 percent of the dalits are practising Hindus. The phenomenon of the cultural assertion of the dalits has till now remained a myth. Hindu critics have long argued that efforts to convert Hindus into Ambedkarite Buddhists are mere political stunts rather than sincere commitment to social reforms. They further argue that the dalit leadership's sectarian agenda has reduced its capacity to enter into a meaningful dialogue with other social groups in order to fast track social reforms. The conversion of dalits into Buddhism has nothing to do with their faith or conviction but it is an act of desperation and frustration. However, according to Dr, Gail Omveldt, "Ambedkar's Buddhism seemingly differs from that of those, who accepted by faith, who go for refuge and accept the cannon. This much is clear from its basis; it does not accept in totality the scriptures of the Theravada, the Mahayana or the Vajrayana. The question that is now clearly put forth: Are there a fourth yana, a Navayana and a kind of modernistic enlightened version of Dhamma really possible within the framework of Buddhism?" Buddhism was supposed to develop into an alternate religious and cultural platform for the dalits from which they could engage with Hinduism on an equal footing without being tied down in any hierarchy. This is yet to happen in contemporary India.

While examining the contemporary Buddhist movement, it can be deduced that the movement is restrictive, limited and is found mainly in urban areas with a sizable neo Buddhist population. The Buddhist social activities are limited to generation of Ambedkarite cultural symbols and making them visible at public places and socio cultural gatherings. Such events are no doubt significant and create social capital but generally, they have ritualistic value and nothing more. The gratification of Buddhist identity can be valuable but it has a narrow audience and hence, it fails to change the attitude of caste Hindus towards the dalits. The Buddhist movement has so far been unsuccessful in creating a strong social strategy by which the non Buddhists can integrate and become harbingers of the social revolution. When we see the growth of the Buddhist movement in Maharashtra, we find that it has been confined only to the Mahar community. The other dalit castes have generally kept themselves away from the movement and these include the Matangs, the Mangs, the Mehtars and the Chambhars. Ambedkar visualized Buddhism as a socio political force to generate a new confidence and moral outlook within the dalits but the disunity among the dalit sub castes and the lack of committed leadership have halted the revolutionary project midstream. The dalit movement in Maharashtra has failed to generate a high pitch cultural assertion that can include the aspirations of all the oppressed groups. They kept talking about ideology and values while, simultaneously, failing in politics. The attempt to bring socio religious changes for the dalits in a constitutionally secular but culturally communal atmosphere through political mobilization had a moral imperative but as a political strategy, it did not yield dividends.

The case in Uttar Pradesh is just the reverse. The BSP has been successful politically but lacks in providing an empowered social set up for the dalits. Incidences of socio economic deprivation for the dalits may be high but despite this, the level of political awareness and mobilization is remarkably top class. It is interesting to know that a major chunk of the electorally powerful dalits has not converted to Buddhism and are practising Hindus. Conversions can have the disastrous effects of the de politisation of communities. A case in this point can be made of the tribals. Despite being 6-8 percent of the population, they are yet to become a politically potent force and have failed to exert any pressure or lobby effectively for the creation of good public policies in their favour. The tribals became victims of the apolitical approach of the nongovernmental organizations. The leadership role came to be assumed by the religious leaders who exhausted all their energies in facilitating and carrying out conversions from one religion to another. The experience of the tribals holds out important lessons for the dalit movement. Embracing Buddhism is not going to culminate in their real emancipation.—at best; it can provide them some solace and lead to cheers among the dalit intelligentsia on the issue of so called cultural assertion of dalits. The religious conversion drive runs the risk of turning the movement apolitical. The high voltage power among the dalits of UP is not due to Buddhism, giving them a separate identity from the Hindus but due to their politicization process. The dalits fought against the forces of Mandal and Hindutva politically. It is no surprise that a clever politician like Mayawati may install Buddhist constructions and name districts after Gautama Buddha and Mahamaya but when it comes to self, she desists from openly claiming herself to be a Buddhist. She is prudent enough to realize that in a country like India where 80 percent of the population is predominantly Hindu, conversion and that too, from Hinduism to another religion, might not go down well with the majority electorate. In a democracy, future of any movement depends upon its electoral clout and only capture of political power can lead to meaningful changes. Fight against Hinduism has less chances of success by parting away from it to form a new alternative but the best course of action seems to be remaining within the system and weakening it from inside.

Dalits have converted to Islam, Sikhism and Christianity to escape from the caste bondage but this has hardly made any difference to their lives. The upper castes who converted to Islam and Christianity have managed to retain the caste tag with them and caste consciousness has crept into the egalitarian ethos of these religions. The dalit Christians are not allowed to have common churches and cemetery grounds with the upper caste Christians. Muslims and Sikhs have also been affected by the caste bug and there are prohibitions on inter caste marriages and inter dining among them. The dalits embraced Sikhism in the hope of gaining social acceptability but their hopes/expectations have been dashed. Social opprobrium continues to affect them as the Jat Sikhs continue to mal treat them both in the gurudwaras and on farm lands. They have been compelled to have separate gurudwaras, marriage halls and cremation places. It is against this backdrop of social exclusion that a large number of dalits are veering away from the mainstream Sikh religion and joining the various deras that have proliferated in Punjab. Another probable cause behind the dalit exodus towards the deras could be the absence of a strong dalit movement in the state. While Hinduism or Hindutva is a form of Brahmanism and intends to suppress the dalit interests, one thing becomes clear that it is not entirely a cultural sort of thing and has to be fought politically.

Coming back to the Hindutva movement, the noticeable trend in it is that post independence, it has mellowed down in its approach to the non caste Hindus because it realized that in order to attain its dream of a pan India united Hindu block, it was imperative to make attempts for unification of Hindu society. The dalits comprising one fifth of our population was a vital cog in the RSS scheme of things and hence the focus shifted towards attempts at social engineering and reconciliation. Today RSS shakhas have been thrown open to the members of the dalit and backward communities. Considering the incendiary nature of reservation issue, the RSS has come to terms with it and jettisoned its earlier stand of opposing the very concept of reservation. Ambedkar has been granted a place in the RSS pantheon and the days of his Jayanti, nirvana and conversion to Buddhism are celebrated with pomp and show by the RSS. Myths of Savari and Nishadhraj Guha have been incorporated from the Ramayana into the Hindutva scheme of things to gain more acceptability from the lower castes. Van Vidyalayas and Shishu Mandir schools have been set up in every nook and corner of the country and their doors have been thrown open to the tribals and the dalits by the RSS with the broad objective of assimilating them into the Hindu fold. Saffronisation of education during the BJP led NDA rule at the centre created controversy as it was felt to be a deliberate move on the part of right wing groups to impose the saffron curriculum over the students in the country. Similar is the furore created due to the attempts of the BJP ruled states to enforce ban on cow slaughter or ask the students to do Surya Namaskar or recite Vande Matram. The BJP has contemplated to undo the tag of being an upper caste party and has co-opted more and more dalits and backward castes within its organization. A dalit politician Bangaru Laxman was made the President of the party and backward caste leaders like Kalyan Singh, Narendra Modi, Uma Bharti and Vinay Katiyaar have managed to shoot into prominence in the party. Though the onward march of the right wing Hindutva forces in the early nineties was checked by the emergence of OBC caste politics that threatened to divide Hinduism, the fact that BJP under the umbrella of NDA captured power can't be ignored. The dalits may have joined hands with mandalites on the reservation bandwagon but the bonhomie between these two votaries of social justice has proved to be ephemeral. Ground level hostilities between the two groups have led to the reconfiguration of societal equations and it does not surprise anyone to see the dalit leadership and the Hindutva forces reading from the same page, at times. Mayawati has become the chief minister of UP thrice with the support of the Hindutva BJP. The dalit movement's flirtation with the right wing continued in Maharashtra with the coming together of the Shiv Shakti and Bhim Shakti alliance. Ram Vilas Paswan, an influential dalit leader from Bihar, accepted a cabinet portfolio during the NDA rule.

These incidents are a grim reminder to the reality that now, Hindutva forces are no longer a taboo for the dalit leadership. Political opportunism is the flavor of the day, rather than durable alliances based on ideological considerations. More ominous signals portend towards the future of the dalit movement. Just reflect what happened in the western state of Gujarat. The involvement of the dalits as the foot soldiers of the Hindutva brigade in the Gujarat riots of 2002 has already caused a flutter in the minds of the dalit intelligentsia. Whatever arguments the dalit intellectuals may give like allurement of the poverty ridden scheduled castes to take RSS sides, the fact remains that today, more and more dalits are getting Hinduised in the state. Participation of the dalits in the 1992 Mumbai riots and the balmikis in the Moradabad riots of UP are incidents that point to the harsh reality that dalits are being pursued and mobilized by the right wing groups in the attainment of their objectives. In Maharashtra, the celebration of the Ganesh Chathurthi festival and carrying out of huge processions with the posse of dalits from the city slums indicate that dalits are now willing to get Hinduised. Even from an electoral point of view, Ambedkar's non conformist/ protestant Hindus are not averse to having occasional flings with the Hindutva forces. The success of the right wing groups in saffronising the myths, legends and minds of the dalits is not because of only a good strategy but also, there is a strong predilection from within the dalit groupings to seek acceptance from the same manuwadis who exploited them and kept them marginalized for centuries. The Hinduisation process is not a one way traffic but a dual process in which, on one hand there is an attempt to seek acceptance of the upper castes while on the other hand, one can find the registering of implicit protest which gets exhibited in the subaltern challenge to the dominant hegemony by becoming one like them.

Now, coming back to the pertinent question—Why is the dalit movement apprehensive of the rise of the Hindutva brigade? What challenge does Hindutva pose to the dalit brigade? From the very inception, the dalit leadership has not been comfortable with the RSS ideology of creating pan India Hindu nationalism because of its exclusive agenda of catering only to the dalit cause. Moreover, the dalit movement is also fearful of the Hindutva's praise for India's past glory and its conviction in the brahminical social structure. Though RSS keeps silent on the issue of reservation nowadays, but their past misgivings on reservation has also added to the element of anxiety in dalit minds. Golwalkar did not take very kindly to the positive affirmative programmes undertaken by the post independent government of India for the welfare of SCs/STs. He expressed his displeasure by stating that the rulers were digging the roots of Hindu social cohesion and destroying the spirit of identity that held various sects into a harmonious whole during the past. He held the constitutional safeguards as creating discord within the Hindu ranks. Dalit activists fear that the RSS surge within the dalit ranks may lead to the loss of dalit social agenda. Certain issues like untouchability, caste based discriminations and reservations are very dear to dalit hearts and it is very likely that these issues do not fire the imagination of the Hindutva forces. Owing to political exigency, the Hindu nationalists may be silent on these issues but deep within; they simmer and are not comfortable with them. **Hindutva talks about common culture, common language, common religion and common ancestry, completely ruling out the existence of autonomous aspirations of the subaltern classes who claim to have a distinct identity and culture from the Hindus.** The all encompassing agenda of Hindutva may subjugate the dalit identity and lead to its submergence within the Hindutva fold and facilitate their becoming cannon fodder of Hinduism. The atrocities committed on the dalits may witness an increase and those dalit groups who refuse to comply with the Hindutva line may be brutalized. The hegemonic and homogenizing influence of the right wing may create hindrance for their overall aspirations of carving out a separate and exclusive dalit constituency, catering to caste based preferences and entitlements. Their so called cultural distinctiveness may also suffer.

The memories of killing of 5 dalits at a place in Haryana, all in the name of holy cow, still rankles in the minds of the dalit activists. The recent ruckus over the beef eating festival at the Osmania University is an indication of the things to come. Hinduisation of the dalits will make the process of dalit assertion much more difficult because the Hinduised dalits will begin to hate their own brethren who are less Hinduised. The dalit leadership has to pay heed to such ominous signs and contemplate the arrest of Hindutva into the dalit fold. The challenge before them is to protect the Ambedkarian legacy of keeping a safe distance from the brahminical Hindutva and at the same time, identifying a new source of socio cultural and spiritual salvation for the dalits. Even the so called partners of the dalit movement in the social justice project are not shying away from jumping on the Hindutva rath and all, in the name of Hindu glory.

Rather than having sleepless nights on how to counter the Hindutva phenomenon, the dalit movement should emulate the example of the Dravidian movement which has managed to keep the Hindutva forces at bay in Tamil Nadu. The social movement, witnessed in the state, led to the political/ social consolidation of the non Brahmin Hindus who managed to counter the Brahmin Hindus effectively. Starting from the atheist plank, the Dravidian movement sought to debrahminise the entire socio political system by advocating for rationalism and humanism and strongly, denouncing caste stratification and ritualism. Non Brahmins were given a chance to become priests of temples to break the monopoly of Brahmins in the conductance of religious ceremonies and moreover, emphasis was laid on the development of Tamil language and culture to counter Sanskrit and Aryan influence. The Tamilian non Brahmins did not look for an alternative religion or a spiritual paradigm to escape oppression from the stratified Hindu society but remained within the ambit of the Hindu religion to challenge it from within; to weaken it from within. **The dalit movement is all about caste solidarity while the Dravidian movement was based on a broader framework involving caste, culture, language and rationality and a reach out policy to all non Brahmins based on principles and convictions, rather than sheer political/vote bank opportunism.**

The dalit leadership/intelligentsia has to prepare proper strategies if it wants to arrest the Hindutva infiltration within its ranks. Hindutva is a mass movement and to counter it, it is essential that instead of depending solely on the urban dalit elites, the dalit movement must strive to form a broad coalition of the vulnerable social groups like scheduled castes, scheduled tribes, extremely backward castes and muslims and try to forge these groups into a common mass front that can challenge the Hindu nationalists. It is not to be forgotten that Hindutva is not a religious movement but a political one and hence it has to be confronted politically. Nothing can come out of religious discourses. The religious conversions of dalits have proved to be illogical and misdirected. Technically, the dalits may have become Buddhists but this has not resulted in their material upliftment or enhancement in their dignity. The prevailing disunity between the dalit and the communist ranks has also abetted the growth of Hindu right wing forces in the country. Despite more than 60 years of the working of our republic, the communists are yet to come to terms with the reality that lies in and around caste. A weak insipid left has provided the space for the Hindu right to grow.

Many political commentators feel that the growth of Hindutva has coincided with the unfolding of the neo reform process in India. Both globalization and Hindutva are complementary and mutually sustain each other. Hence while fighting against the Hindutva hegemony; the dalit movement should also simultaneously rebel against the forces of globalization and economic imperialism. Neo liberalism has given birth to fundamentalist and fascist forces with its emphasis on the individual and autonomy of market and that too, sans morality and ethics. Capitalists, bureaucrats, industrialists, upper castes, intermediate castes, middle class, rich farmers etc all are proponents of Hindutva; they can be challenged by the dalits on the streets but let's ponder what happens after that? The state comes to their rescue.

There is also another dimension to the growth of Hindutva as a political movement. The 1990s saw the implementation of the Mandal Commission Report that laid the basis for the empowerment and political consolidation of the backward castes. Mandalisation of the polity led to cracks and fissures in the Hindu society; the Hindu unity was in tatters with both the OBCs and the upper castes at daggers drawn with each other. Fault lines emerged within the internal organization of almost all the mainstream political parties which were compelled to induct backward castes into the top most positions in their party hierarchies. The proponents of Hindutva knew that until and unless they forge a common united Hindu front cutting across caste barriers, the chances of their survival was slim. The top most Hindutva leadership comprised of mostly the upper castes and that too, in a country where OBCs accounted for around half of the population. LK Advani embarked on the rath Yatra, talked of Hindu pride and began to mobilize public opinion for the construction of the Ram Temple at Ayodhya. Kamandal was pitted against Mandal. The basic motive of the BJP leadership was to check the Mandal onslaught and prevent the disintegration of Hindu society on caste lines.

Reservation: the never ending syndrome

India is perhaps the only example of any democracy where reservation in public employment is given to the majority community, with SC/ST/OBCs comprising 80 percent of the population. Here the generals want to become backwards, the backwards long for reservation under SC category and the SCs want to have the tag of STs. This has made our nation the laughing stock of the world. No doubt, reservation has increased the representation of the scheduled castes in government jobs and legislatures but this arrangement is not something that has to continue till eternity. The constitution makers had hoped that after attaining its purpose of making bureaucracy more diverse and representative, reservation would be done away with. With the spread of education, welfare and development, it was assumed that there will be a gradual decline in the volume or quantum of reservation. However, just the reverse has happened—reservation increased in its scope and extent. With the implementation of reservation policy for the OBCs in public employment and educational institutes, India is fast becoming a republic where populist and vote bank politics matter more than the genuine welfare of the people. Names of the communities under OBC/SC/ST lists are more a matter of politics and pampering than the realization of the need to improve their socio economic status. The number of constitutional castes has far outnumbered the number of castes mentioned in the Dharamshastras. Reservation seems to have become the panacea to all the problems relating to backwardness of the communities. According to the vision of the founding fathers of our constitution, reservation was the means to achieve the end and the end was the upliftment of the marginalized communities by increasing their representation in administration and legislatures. However, in this age of competitive politics, reservation seems to have become the end in itself. Marathas are a socially dominant and powerful community in Maharashtra but they want reservation at par with the OBCs. The Jats, a prosperous farming community of western UP, Haryana and Punjab have benefitted immensely from the Green Revolution, riding on the crest of huge government subsidies but they are desperate for getting reservation. They are in agitation mode and are out on the streets. The Gujjars are one step ahead—they want to get the tag of STs so that they can get on to the same pedestal as the Meenas of Rajasthan. The Meenas have made the most of the reservation benefits provided to them. Today, there is hardly any Indian state where this community is not having a good presence in IAS/IPS cadre but despite this, they want reservation for them to continue. They are averse to the very idea of being excluded from the ST list and hence their violent clashes with the Gujjars community. In the backdrop of such demands, the biggest casualty seems to be our fledgling democracy. A democracy promising equality of opportunity seems to have been caught into a dilemma.

Though a strong proponent of positive affirmative action programmes in favour of the downtrodden marginalized communities, Ambedkar never wanted reservation to continue beyond a certain time frame but unfortunately, today reservation runs the risk of becoming a permanent feature of our polity. Concession once given has now become a right. Reservation culminates in unbridgeable social identities and thus, has the deleterious consequence of weakening the national integrating forces. Though it was enforced to compensate for the sins of past caste based discriminations, it may degenerate into some sort of a reverse discrimination. It has failed to achieve its ultimate objective of creation of a just and egalitarian social order. For the politicians, it has become an effective instrument to pander to its constituency and hence the road to possible short cut success. The dalits have lagged in all the socio economic indices and development parameters. A good percentage of their population lack access to safe drinking water and more than 50 percent of the dalit children under the age of 5 years are malnourished and have stunted growth. Avenues of quality education and good healthcare facilities are not available to them. Majority of the young children can't attend schools on a regular basis as their parents need their services for increasing the household income to make both their ends meet. More than 60 percent of the dalit population lives in villages and are engaged in agriculture either as landless labourers or as petty, impoverished marginal farmers. These pressing problems confronting the dalits are beyond the radar screen of the dalit movement because they are too preoccupied with the reservation issue and think only it can solve their problems. **The stark reality is that reservation has only provided crutches to**

the dalits; it has not healed them completely. It has acted in a detrimental manner to the cause of the dalit movement as the perception of the dalits being parasites and the ones that thrive on state charity is fast gaining ground. The oft repeated refrain of most of the non dalits is that the dalit activists talk of historical atrocities committed on them and play the victim card just to gain sympathy and secure concessions from the state. Whatever arguments that the dalit leadership/intelligentsia make in favour of reservation do not carry much water as the original intention of reservation was to bring the dalits on the same level as the non dalits in terms of socio economic development and then terminate it. This concept was necessitated due to the long years of humiliation and subjugation suffered by the lower caste population which led to their stunted socio economic development, low representation in public offices and high indices of deprivation levels.

Today, BSP and dalit intelligentsia/activists are up in arms against the UPA Government at the centre for not being able to get the constitutional amendment bill facilitating reservation in promotion in government jobs for the dalits passed. Surprisingly, despite the reservation demand in promotion being struck down by the Supreme Court, it was the National Democratic Alliance that brought in three constitutional amendments in between 2000 to 2002 paving way for reservation not only in promotion but also in consequential seniority. In 2006, the Supreme Court went by Nagraj case which stressed on taking into account not only inadequacy of representation in the services and backwardness of SC/STs but also the efficiency of administration. It was this case that the Supreme Court took note in 2012 while upholding the Allahabad High Court judgement striking down the quota provisions of SC/STs in promotions brought in by the erstwhile Mayawati Government in the state of Uttar Pradesh. The Union Government's (UPA) attempts to bring in quota provisions for the dalits may run into rough weather in the form of the hurdle in the judiciary. Hence, to escape from judicial scrutiny, article 16 (4) may be tampered with to delete the clause "inadequacy of representation" and Article 335 may be modified to delete "efficiency in administration" clause. Time and again, the ruling dispensions find it very difficult to prove the extent of backwardness of these deprived communities due to lack of effective and proper survey and hence it can't prove its case for reservation in promotions for them. This may tempt the government to do away with the need to determine the extent of backwardness clause.

Parties like the Samajwadi are opposing the passage of the constitutional amendment bill facilitating reservation for the SC/STs in promotions not out of any genuine concern for the non dalits but for the simple reason that they want similar provisions for the OBCs. The plea, which they are offering to oppose the move, is that once implemented, this provision will adversely affect the general candidates, does not cut much ice considering their track record in such matters. The political parties know that the dalits and the OBCs are in a majority and hence, they feel no compunction in pandering to their unjustified demands if that boosts their electoral prospects. Don't be surprised if tomorrow the 50 percent ceiling imposed on reservation in government jobs by the judiciary is done away with, in keeping with the kind of vote bank politics that is played in India and the ever increasing demands from various communities.

Reservation at the entry point is understandable as it brings two persons on an equal footing but extending this to upward career progression is not fair as it is tantamount to giving preference to one over the other, based on caste factors, even though both of them are at the same pedestal. Many states like Karnataka and Tamil Nadu have enacted legislations to enable reservations beyond the judicially prescribed ceilings of 50 percent reservation and not only this; they have managed to insulate this with the help of the Centre via Schedule1X of the constitution to escape from judicial scrutiny. Age relaxations and increase in number of attempts for appearing in job related examinations for the reserved class of citizens, have seriously undermined the very rationale of this concept. This manifests the extent to which the political leadership can stoop low to cater to petty vote bank politicking, irrespective of the rule of law and principles of equality and fraternity. The pro reservationists have managed to subvert our democracy into a cartel of vested interests where premium is put on mediocrity, rather than meritocracy and stress is laid on representation, rather than competition. **The tyranny of democracy gets manifested in cases where policies are not framed in accordance with the national goals or the spirit of the constitution but to cater to the interests of the dominant electorally powerful communities who seem to be more concerned with sharing the spoils of power.**

The anti reservationists are the favorite whipping boys of the political class as they lack the numbers to have an effective say in this increasingly dalit/OBC dominated polity. The upper caste politicians prefer to keep quiet as the upper castes are not in a position to ensure their victory at the elections. **The famous word in the Indian political dictionary is "social justice" which is nothing but a euphemism for the perpetration of politics of caste, caste based entitlements and caste identity solidarity.** Reservation was born from the womb of social justice which, perhaps, seems to be the least understood word in Indian political lexicon. The proponents of reservation argue that the imperatives of social justice mandate that the growth process should be distributive and reach all the segments of the population. There are others who contend that reservation is not a poverty alleviation programme and has got nothing to do with the reduction of poverty or upliftment of the quality of life. The main purpose of reservation is to break the monopoly of the upper castes in our bureaucratic and political structures and increase the participation of dalits/OBCs in them. The pro reservationists feel that there is no point in identifying the creamy layer among the reserved categories because it is a divisive ploy on the part of the ruling class to create dissensions with the dalit and OBC ranks. The basic assumption behind such a stand is that the OBCs/dalits once selected to strategic bureaucratic/administrative positions would ensure that their fellow brethren are not victimized and their interests are adequately taken care of. But has this assumption come true? Participation of dalits and backwards has increased but has this increase in participation been meaningful? Participation, though desirable, can't be the end goal of any positive affirmative action plan until and unless it leads to betterment in the socio economic life of the stakeholders. **Participation can't be end neutral and doesn't take place in a vacuum; representation/participation is there to make the system more inclusive and cater to the needs and aspirations of various groups.** The founding fathers of our constitution did not want the participation or representation to be confined to a few select privileged groups, generation after generation, but wanted the participation process to disperse evenly and empower even the marginalized groups at the grass root level.

It is true that a few thousand odd public jobs in a year can't lead to any appreciable change in the quality of life of the reserved classes but at least, it sets the empowerment process in motion. And by the way, what have the better off dalits and backwards, after taking the benefits of reservation, done for their fellow caste men? Are their attitudes any different from the upper castes or the intermediate castes in the performance of their duties? Just as the upper castes have tended to maintain their supremacy in the social set up, the privileged dalits and backwards have done the same to their fellow brethren by turning a blind eye to their predicament. The privileged ones have ensured that the marginalized sections within their own groups remain voiceless without having a share in the state benefits. As can be witnessed in several states that have had backward caste assertion, the attitude of the backwards towards the dalits have been more deplorable than the upper castes. The well off sections within the dalits and the backwards have picked up the attitudes and mannerisms of the upper castes and don't be surprised if you find them more Brahmin than the Brahmin themselves.

Social justice has become a buzzword. Many parties, especially the regional ones, practice blatant casteism and are adherents to the principle of primogeniture, but despite this, they are condoned for the sake of social justice. They indulge in corruption and yet escape unscathed due to dalliances with the ruling party or parties in a coalition as the social justice plank shields them. They may have picked up the letters of the constitution to suit their designs but they have failed to imbibe the spirit of the constitution. A number of parties confined at the regional levels like the Samajwadi Party, Bahujan Samaj Party, Rashtriya Janata Dal, Janata Dal United, DMK etc. all have based their politics on the so called social justice plank that entails identifying their constituencies, contemplating to prove these sections of population as underrepresented and socio economically backward and demand, if possible, get reservation for them. Since India is an amalgam of various castes and communities, any feasible electoral alliance seeks merger of more than one community together, the consolidated reservation demands climb up. Social justice of the indigenous variety encourages competitive reservation demands and opens competitive bidding of certain communities to press for their demands. This is fine to some extent but what if demands for reservation are guided more by politics than genuine reasons of under representation and socio economic backwardness.

Representation of backwards & dalits is welcome but what would be the repercussions if this representation or participation doesn't lead to an improvement in the quality of life of the suffering masses and is mere symbolic, rather than substantial?

Social justice or to be precise, say reservation, is too broad an issue to be confined only to the caste issue. The structure of our society is conspicuously marked by overlapping inequalities that may not be linked to any dominant caste or community identity. Take the case of 7-8 percent of our population who are disabled/ handicapped in varying organs and to varying degrees. What do you say about the huge displaced adivasis/dalit population, uprooted from their homes by capitalistic plunder?

Social justice has refused to express itself in any other form, other than reservations. Granting of reservations to promote social justice seems to be the only remedy available to the political parties, championing the cause of social justice. However, there are limits to the utility of social justice that is practiced in India.

The drafting of constitution, sometimes referred to as the social contract of the dalits with the state, mandalisation of the polity post 1990, vociferous demands from various communities to get reservation benefits and the gradual increase in the list of castes included under SC/ST/OBC, immense electoral prospects linked to mobilization of one or more communities and the reluctance of the mainstream parties dominated traditionally by the upper castes to speak anything against reservation—all these are manifestations of the clout/power of social justice politics. **But this does not mean that this brand of politics remains unchallenged in India. A plateau**

has been reached from where the law of diminishing return has set in. The LPG (Liberalisation, Privatisation & Globalisation) phase has only hastened the downslide. More and more job openings are now available in the sectors, outside government, in private companies, multinationals, nongovernmental organizations etc. This has effectively tied the hands of successive governments in India to increase the width and scope of reservation and the fact that most of the political parties, barring the left, are in agreement to varying degrees with the ongoing economic reforms, leaves hardly any space for the current scenario to change. Then take the case of Reservation in Promotion for the SC/STs constitutional amendment bill, what happened? The Bill failed to get going because parties like Samajwadi Party opposed it tooth and nail. DMK was not enthusiastic about it. Interestingly, both the parties rode to power on the wave of social justice. Even some sections within the dominant national parties like the Congress and the BJP, though not vocal for political reasons, were against the bill. There have been cases in the past where reservation concept has been subverted and its underlying essence battered where in the name of filling backlog vacancies; seats meant for dalits have been given to the general candidates. Now, let's move to Mandal 2, i.e. reservation for OBC students in higher education. While the nitty gritty of the Act is yet to be clearly worked out to benefit the OBC students, the general category students are making hay while the sun is shining in the form of creation of additional seats to compensate for the loss caused to general category students. Some backward caste parties supposedly harbingers of social justice are now openly calling for repealing of SC/ST act. **Rifts and fault lines are appearing within the OBC/dalit groups and there have been calls for reservation within reservation based on sub classification of various reserved categories.**

The BSP and other dalit parties are beset by an ideological vacuum. OBC dominated parties are now realizing their limits, their political ambitions are contained and more or less, they are resigned to their fates of localized bases. So naturally, the aggression that marked Mandal 1 seemed to be lacking in Mandal 2. Moreover, they have become defensive due to lack of conviction on their part and the ability of the no reservation lobby to occupy the moral high ground. Military and judiciary continue to remain outside the pale of reservation and so are the highly scientific technical expertise services. So may be, in the coming years, we see a decline in the potential of social justice to be effectively used as a mobilizing or gluing factor.

There is animated talk in the academic circles about the changing dimensions of the empowerment process. The Social Justice plank laid emphasis on the handing out of state positive affirmative action plans to the backward marginalized social groups like reservation based on the assumption that only state knows what is good for them. The beneficiaries are assumed to be passive recipients of state dole outs. The beneficiaries become totally dependent on the state and lose the incentive or the inner urge to develop themselves. This results in their retarded development. Now, the new emerging thought about empowerment is that the state can't be the doer but it has to act as the facilitator. The marginalized groups should be given a stake in the development process and their participation has to be there at various levels starting from policy formulation to policy implementation to policy evaluation. They need to have a say in the making of decisions that have an impact on their daily lives. They should not be treated as passive and must be encouraged to develop themselves. Investment must be made in their HRD so that they get opportunities to make choices from the environment; the choices may be political, economic, social or any other.

At a time, when sweeping changes are taking place in the world with the focus on liberalization, privatization and globalization and the trend is towards the receding role of the state in the realm of the market and governance, it remains to be seen whether state reservation is relevant today. The private sector/ the multinational corporations are not bound by any constitutional obligations to provide job security to the dalits/backwards. Moreover, there is a fierce competition within the corporate world where only the fittest survive. The number of job opportunities in the public sector is declining rapidly. Add to it, the apathy of the corporate sector towards the charter of social responsibility. What lies ahead on the road for the dalit activists? The new economic reforms have already integrated the Indian economy with the global economy and they can't be undone or wished away. The most viable option for the dalit leadership/intelligentsia under the present circumstances is to lay stress on the need for quality education and capacity building of the dalits to prepare them for taking on globalization as a challenge and not something, that has been superimposed on them by the oft repeated Manuwadi forces. But this requires painstaking efforts and hence, the dalit movement does not give any emphasis on this. Already vociferous demands have emanated from various dalit quarters, asking for reservation in the private sector.

More than 60 years of reservation has led to the emergence of a new class of dalits which has managed to corner most of the reservation benefits. This neo dalit class is the most ardent supporter of caste based reservation. Sanskritisation of dalits and the co-optation of this neo class into the system gave rise to a bourgeoisie class of elite dalits. This empowered dalit class colluded with the dalit leadership and intelligentsia to usurp the agenda of the dalit movement. Even Ambedkar had lamented the rise of this class who after attaining power and prosperity forgot their own brethren and began to identify themselves with the upper castes. Time and again, they too suffer from the stigma, attached with being born in a low caste but in course of time, they have managed to forge a confluence of interests with the upper caste elites. Ambedkarism for them is a mere symbol, not an ideology that has to be internalized in hearts. Ambedkar is remembered only on his birthdays or nirvana days while the rest of the year is spent in personal aggrandizement by them. This neo dalit class continues to play the sectarian card as and when needed, to suit their nefarious designs of the social balkanization of the country. It is this self seeking and opportunistic class, way ahead of the common dalit masses in the development pyramid that is leading the movement.

Most of the dalits are born in independent India where a broad consensus exists on the needs of an equal and egalitarian society. The old feudal set up is gradually eroding, urbanization is galloping and more social intercourse is taking place between the dalits and the non dalits. There is a secular legislature, secular executive, secular judiciary, the walls of caste discrimination are slowly crumbling and there is more and more sharing of public space between the dalits and the non dalits. Though the social transformation has been gradual, it is visible now.

Reservation has outlived its utility now and has not made the desired impact as it should have. It has led to a rat race among various castes and communities, with each of them trying to outdo each other in getting the tag of backwardness. The politicians seem to have run out of ideas to offer concrete solutions to bridge the gap between various sections of the population. Hence, apart from the readymade solution of reservation, they can't think of any other alternative. Though the real intention behind the concept of reservation was genuine and justified to a good extent, the harsh reality is that it is still out of bounds for majority of the dalit population. A privileged minority within the dalits are usurping all the benefits while the majority is excluded from the benefits. Day to day problems of the dalit masses do not stir the imagination of the dalit leadership or the intelligentsia as does reservation. **It's high time the creamy layer within the dalit community be identified and excluded from the ambit of reservation. If the creamy layer concept can be followed in the implementation of OBC reservation, there is no reason why the dalit movement should see red at the very mention of creamy layer within the dalit community. If this does not seem feasible, then why not restrict dalit**

reservation to one or two generations in a family? If that happens, a lot of opportunities can be generated for the left out groups within the dalit community in the sphere of education and public employment. The social growth process will be deepened, become more inclusive and a common dalit will stand to benefit. A rural dalit working as a daily labourer on an agricultural field can't be expected to get a good job in any government department as he does not fulfill the educational eligibility criteria to even apply for the job, leave alone getting selected. Only those dalits are reaping the benefits of reservation who are educated and placed higher up in terms of development indicators. The Employment of Manual Scavengers and Construction of Dry Latrines (Prohibition) Act though passed by the Parliament way back in 1993, still remains largely on paper and even today, it is not rare to find lower caste people doing manual scavenging works and leading a sub human existence. The dalit leadership does not think about them; the concerns of the children of those dalits with regards to health and nutritional levels and even primary education are seldom noticed. If more than half the populations of dalits residing in remote far flung rural areas or even urban slums of the nation are helpless in enabling their children to complete even primary level education, leave alone graduation/higher education, what chances they stand in competing with their fellow brethren who are more privileged? The dalit leadership is with the minority—the privileged neo dalit class who are not willing to share their cake with the less fortunate dalits. This is amply demonstrated by the failure of the movement in identifying the better off dalits and calling for their de reservation thus creating the impression that it has got nothing to do with the overall welfare of the dalits.

Coming back to the issue of reservation in promotion, the dalit leadership keeps carping on the low representation of the dalits on top most bureaucratic levels like the secretary to the government of India or principal secretaries of various departments at state levels. No one can deny the fact that the sole reason for this is not the prevailing prejudice or bias against the dalit bureaucrats but there is also another valid reason for this. Age relaxations have been provided to the dalit candidates and as a natural corollary to this is the fact that a considerable percentage of dalits join the services after attaining the age of 30 years. Since the age of superannuation for both the dalits and the non dalits is the same, it comes as no surprise that a majority of dalit bureaucrats retire before reaching the top echelons of office. So, the logical course of action seems to be either raising the retirement age of dalit bureaucrats or removing the age relaxations for dalits and then, giving them reservation in promotions. **Retaining the age relaxation clause and then, implementing reservation in promotion does not look reasonable. But unfortunately, the dalit leadership suffers from idea deficit and talking about the logic of reservation in front of them is synonymous to showing a red rag to a bull.**

It is time to revisit the concept of reservation. The motive behind it should be to modify it and make it in consonance with the changing socio economic realities of the country. Reservation, as a source of empowerment, has been successful to some extent but overall, it has failed to benefit the majority of the deprived class. The driving mantra behind reservation has been to empower the weaker sections of our society but the burning question today is—has empowerment taken place? Empowerment implies enabling the deprived communities to take control over their environment—social, cultural, political and economic. For this, it is imperative to invest in their HRD so that they get better educational and healthcare facilities. This will, in turn, lead to more choices and alternatives before them in making decisions. The process of empowerment is not one dimensional and should not been seen only in terms of reservation. Empowerment can't be imposed from above by the political executive until and unless the deprived communities are willing to empower themselves. **The irony is that today, more and more communities want to become the passive beneficiaries of state action by getting reservation, oblivious to the fact that real development can only happen by active engagement with the state and becoming partners in development and decision making that affect their lives. The nation needs a vibrant debate on the various facets of empowerment.**

Dalit movement: Amidst contradictions and sub groups

The dalit movement has failed to lend cohesiveness to the aspirations of the dalit masses. At present, the scheduled caste population comprises more than 200 sub castes and spatially, the dalit population is well dispersed throughout the length and breadth of the country. Punjab has the largest percentage of dalit population at around 30-31 percent of the entire population of the state. States like Bihar, west Bengal, Tamil Nadu, Uttar Pradesh and Andhra Pradesh together constitute around 60 percent of the total scheduled caste population of the country. **Some major dalit castes had a head start over other dalit castes owing to their superior educational and economic status and hence, the advantages of reservation and political representation were not evenly distributed.** These empowered dalit castes derived disproportionate benefits, in comparison to their population and ultimately, hijacked the dalit agenda thus marginalizing the other less empowered dalit communities, in the process.

A case in this point can be made of UP, the most populous state in the Indian union. Here, the dalits are divided into 66 castes. Of them, the cobbler castes, the Pasis, the Jatavs and the Koris are conspicuous while Jogis, Nats, Doms, Mushahars and Domars are not visible. Politically, the cobbler castes are well organized. Because of better education, most of the reserved scheduled caste seats go to them in government jobs and educational institutions. The other dalit castes like the Nats, Mushahars and Doms have not produced strong popular leaders and so, their voices lie suppressed. They lack in human development indices and their plight is no better than the untouchables of pre independence years. In Bihar, the cobbler castes and the paswans have managed to corner most of the reservation benefits, leaving the other dalit communities into wilderness. Jagjivan Ram and Ram Vilas Paswan, the two prominent faces of Bihar, belonged to cobbler and paswan communities, respectively.

Now, let us take a look at some recent developments. Chinks have surfaced in the armoury of the dalit movement. Today, the uneven level of development and empowerment among the various dalit castes and the marginalization of certain groups among the dalits have led to a chorous among them demanding sub classification of dalits. The first phase of dalit empowerment was marked by demand for reservation of dalits in public employment and the second phase advocates micro based identity demands i.e. sub reservation for various dalit castes within the overall reservation scheme of dalits within constitutionally mandated ceiling of 15 percent for the scheduled castes. Fissures are already widening and the myth of a compact, homogenous identity is being busted. Reports of conflicts between mahars and matangs in Maharashtra, malas and madigas in Andhra Pradesh and cobbler castes and bhangis in UP are already emanating from varied sources. In Punjab, despite a substantial presence, the dalits have not been able to pose a threat to the Congress or the Akalis electorally. Why? If we examine the reasons for this, we find that the dalits do not present a united front and tend to drift in different directions. Their unity was already broken when the Congress Government under the chief ministership of Giani Zail Singh in the 1970s, reserved 50 percent government jobs for Valmikis and the Majhabi Sikhs within the mandated ceiling of scheduled caste reservation. This was done intentionally to weaken the hold of the dominant social group Ravidasis/cobbler castes over government jobs. Not only this, it was necessary to bridge the widening disparities in terms of living conditions between the valmikis/majhabis and the ravidasis/cobbler castes. Haryana followed suit in 1994 by dividing the scheduled caste reservation into two halves cobbler castes and non cobbler castes.

Let us come to Andhra Pradesh. In this state, there are around 60 castes within the scheduled caste population. The level of socio economic disparity within these communities is glaring. Some of the dalit castes have managed to improve their quality of life owing to political clout and benefits from the state while the left out groups are still groveling under acute and distressing levels of poverty. Considering this, a committee under Raju Ram Chandra was formed to study the situation and come up with appropriate recommendations. The committee concluded that there is disproportionate distribution of reservation benefits in favour of Mala and the Adi Andhra Group, compared to their population and both the Madagi and Relli group of communities are not adequately represented. Accordingly, the state government passed the Andhra Pradesh Rationalization of Reservation Act 2000 after accepting the recommendations of Raju Ram Chandra Commission Report. The dalit leaders of the state protested at this perceived attempt of the state government to divide the scheduled caste population and matters reached the apex court. In its 2004 verdict, the Supreme Court declared the act as unconstitutional and stated that the sub classification of the dalit population violated Article 14.

For the time being, the SC verdict may have prevented the sub classification plan of the dalits from taking shape but the genie is out of the bottle. This demand is not going to end and in the near future, there is every possibility of this issue coming to the fore again. The dalit leadership can't afford to adopt an ostrich like approach and must endeavour to find a way out of this impasse in favour of the marginalized dalit castes. Several non dalit politicians are rubbing their hands with glee at the increasing schisms within dalit ranks. Social equations within the dalit community do not reflect an overall solidarity with the aims/objectives of the dalit movement as the general feeling is that the electorally powerful dalit communities are making merry at the expense of their less privileged brethren. Taking advantage of the situation of prevailing internal squabbles within the dalit ranks, the Nitish Kumar Government in Bihar created a special category of Mahadalits within the dalits for specifically introducing state measures to uplift their socio economic status. The dalit politicians were caught napping initially, but then realizing the game plan of the Nitish Government, they began protesting. Even the National Commission for SCs has termed this act of the state government as unconstitutional but the state has refused to budge. **It was pretty obvious that the Mahadalits didn't get their constitutional due, were languishing in misery and were given a raw deal at the hands of the state dalit leadership who seemed to be too preoccupied with their personal vaunting ambitions and had no time to think about the requirements of the impoverished dalit masses.**

The dalit leadership/intelligentsia look at the demands of sub categorization, followed by sub reservation according to this categorization, as a sinister attempt on the part of the brahminical forces to break the dalit solidarity for securing their political ends. They can't be faulted for this as history has been a witness to several occasions when the ruling parties have indulged in blatant display of divide and rule policy in this age of increasingly fierce competitive politics. The dalits have been at the receiving end of these game plans in the past. But at the same time, the dalit leadership has to do some serious soul searching as to why the dalits have been left vulnerable to such type of machinations on the part of other political formations? Why the monolithic dalit entity is showing fault lines and fissures? It is always an easy option to put the blame on others and castigate them but this option, at times, leads to political hara-kiri. Is it not true that the dalit society has become more and more unequal, despite more than 60 years of reservation with the already poor among them driven to the state of hopelessness and despair? The privileged reservation beneficiaries have assumed the leadership mantle and have perpetrated the same injustice to the overall aspirations of the dalit masses as the so called manuwadi forces. Far from being a weapon of socio economic emancipation of dalits, reservation has degenerated into a tool to propagate one's well being for the dalit elites. The end is not socio economic but political. A Mayawati scoffs at the plan of the Congress to have sub quotas for different sub castes among the dalit community within the prescribed ceiling of 15 percent, to enable the benefits to be dispersed equitably. National Commission on Scheduled Castes blasts Nitish Kumar's Maha dalit Commission as unconstitutional. The Supreme Court decision may have saved the dalit movement from being witness to the fragmentation of dalit community but the writing is clear on the wall. The dalit leadership has not managed to get its act together and it has been guilty of ignoring the socio economic aspirations and welfare of the marginalized dalit sub sections who have not gained anything from decades of reservation. **Only that movement sustains that puts common interests above individual interests. Can the dalit leadership pay heed to selfless struggle of Ambedkar for the dalit cause or just be content to put self before the common scheduled caste masses?** After all one can't turn a blind eye to the observation of the Kelkar Committee that services were not meant for the servants but for the services of the society as a whole. As we have discussed above, some state governments have already fragmented the dalit identity and divided it into sub groups, each having separate quotas within the consolidated 15 percent ceiling for dalits.

Just consider the logic of reservation. The dalits and the OBCs were given reservation to increase their representation in public employment and legislatures. This act has arguably led to the development and genuine empowerment of both the groups. Previously, both the dalits and the OBCs were excluded from the development/empowerment process and this culminated in the stunting of their growth potential. Both these groups are very large and together they constitute more than 70 percent of the population. Add to it the fact that they are not homogenous and are divided into hundreds of sub groups which do not have uniform level of development and empowerment. The welfare state has a social responsibility towards the weak and the excluded. **If social justice has been a catchword in Indian polity, why not take it to its logical conclusion and ensure that the fruits of development and positive state affirmative programmes reach the poorest of the poor?** To identify and locate the weaklings, a survey should be carried out as the sub classification of the dalits/ backwards has become a socio economic and political reality and this seems to be the only way to reach out to the excluded sections within the reserved categories. The dalit leadership's slogan of dalit solidarity sounds hollow until and unless, it creates a just and equitable distribution of resources. A movement, speaking the language of a mere 10-20 percent of the dalits can't be genuine. It lacks the perspective and the credibility factor. **The social justice plank appears farcical if it takes note of only the macro identity factors and leaves the issue of micro identity unattended.**

If the dalit movement does not come to terms with the sub classification plan for the dalits for a more equitable distribution of resources, it can go for another alternative. This alternative can raise the hackles of the dalit leadership and intelligentsia but nevertheless, it can be worth experimenting. The caste based sectarian reservation system should be abrogated. The movement has to show the farsightness and call for reservation on secular considerations. The reservation can be based on a deprivation index encompassing dimensions like income, access to healthcare/education/drinking water/ proper sanitation and housing and special category like the physically challenged. If it is not possible to exclude caste as one of the factors determining the level of backwardness due to political reasons, it can be made as one of the factors in determining the level of deprivation index, apart from the above mentioned secular factors. Even if the reservation criteria become more secular, the dalit community will not be the loser. Statistics reveal that more than 50 percent of the dalit population lives below the poverty line and lack access to the basic requirements of life. More than 60 percent of the dalit children suffer from malnutrition. Naturally, the number of scheduled caste people benefitting from such sort of a reservation policy will be more. The only hindrance may be the proper identification of the beneficiaries but if the beneficiary selection process is linked to the Unique Identification Card Scheme of the government along with the involvement of the local elected body, the chances of fairness in the whole exercise increases. The volume of reservation benefits of the dalits may increase, considering the level of backwardness prevailing among the dalits. Also demand for quality education and provision of better healthcare facilities can go a long way in raising the quality of life, rather than remaining stuck in reservation. Acceptance of the new reservation model can foster better relations between the dalits and the non dalits resulting in the burial of the age long animosity between them. Moreover, political brinkmanship will die a natural death and the nation will not have to suffer the ignominy of caste based reservation demands in its supposedly secular/inclusive architecture. For Ambedkar, political equality for the dalits has to be accompanied by socio economic equality with the non dalits for the healthy growth of our democracy. Reservation has failed to have a trickledown effect among the dalits and has created an abyss between the have and have nots of the community. Leave aside the parity issue with the non dalits, even within them, there is no parity. Reservation for Ambedkar was a temporary constitutional obligation of the state towards the dalits, having validity till the date the dalits come to the same level as the non dalits. It was not a right for the dalits but a positive state affirmative programme. Reservation continues to linger on and fester, not because it is needed but because the leaders want to retain it.

Dalit movement and the issue of land

One of the facts of the movement that has blunt its edge is that it is spearheaded by a short sighted urban based dalit bourgeoisie and the representation of common rural dalits in it is miniscule. Over the last decades, around 15-20 percent of these urban dalits have taken over the dalit agenda and are obsessed with the single issue of reservation. This is a clear indication of the urban and class bias of the movement that has repeatedly ignored issues relating to rural dalits. Reservation had benefits for the first generation dalits but now, it has become an exclusive prerogative of the few. According to National Sample Survey Office data 2003-2004, one third of all the rural households are landless and to compound the woes, a further one third of rural households possess marginal or little land less than 0.4 hectares. The next 20 percent hold land less than one hectare. In other words, 60 percent of the population has rights over only 5 percent of the country's land, whereas 10 percent of the population has control over 55 percent of the land resources. Today, the growing realization is that the previous land reform policy failed to reap the requisite benefits due to the structural inequities in our socio political set up. Caste, class and patriarchy converged with political and bureaucratic systems to defeat the social distributive plank of land reforms. Despite this, the dalit activists and leadership fail to realize the merits of the case.

Dalits have been traditionally dispossessed of land assets and hence their inferior status in society. Caste is linked to skewed/unequal distribution or landlessness of the dalits. Ambedkar realized this from the very beginning and urged his supporters to take to land struggles in Marathwada in the state of Maharashtra. Dada Saheb Gaikwad, an Ambedkarite was instrumental in leading many country wide land struggles. The Congress Socialist Party was formed by the leading socialists like Narendra Dev, Lohia, Ashok Mehta and JP Narayan. Though they were in the fold of Congress initially, their advocacy for land reforms fell on deaf ears and ultimately, they broke away from the Congress to give shape to their socialist vision. Independent India with its welfare orientation realized the need for land reforms, in tune with its socialist vision of creation of an equal society with equitable distribution of resources. Several socially progressive legislations were passed like the Land Tenancy Acts, the Zamindari Abolition Act and the Land Ceiling Act. These reforms were aimed at carrying out a major transformation of rural landscape by giving land rights to the actual tillers of the land. The social dominance of the landed class was sought to be whittled down by the imposition of the land ceiling acts to facilitate the fragmentation of their holdings in favour of the marginalized landless communities. Voluntary land donation movements were launched by the likes of Vinoba Bhave to persuade the landed farmers to give land to the poor people. However, the land reform movement was not fully successful due to the lack of political will and the collusion between the rich farmers/landed class and the politicians of the ruling party, most of whom belonged to the upper/intermediate castes. Large farmers gained from numerous exemptions such as to charitable trusts and religious trusts most of which were bogus or on paper only. They handed out tracts of lands to their kith and kin; let go only their marginal lands and often continued to retain possession of their benami lands. The lands continued to be cultivated by the socially powerful groups and allotments to dalits remained largely on paper as allotees were forcefully evicted and not allowed to take possession of lands. There is no official data even of the extent of dalit land alienation, leave alone restoration of land to them. Tenancy provisions were also grossly distorted in repossessing land for personal cultivation, large scale eviction of tenants from their lands, collusion with local revenue authorities to make sure that their tenancy was not recorded and even forceful eviction of legal right holders even after the transfer of legal titles to them.

These land reforms were aimed at carrying out a major transformation of rural landscape by giving land rights to the actual tillers of the land. The social dominance of the landed class was sought to be whittled down by the imposition of the land ceiling acts to facilitate the fragmentation of their holdings in favour of the marginalized landless communities. However whatever benefits accrued from the land reforms went to the powerful OBC communities who later onwards, with the onset of Green Revolution, Community Development Extension Programmes and Cooperative Societies, increased their economic status and socio political clout. The dalits were excluded from the entire process and land assets continued to elude them. The original intent of the reforms was lost. This contributed to be one of the reasons for the rise of Naxalism in Jharkhand, Bihar, Andhra Pradesh and certain pockets of central India. CPI (ML), CPI (UNITY) and MCC flourished in Jharkhand, central India and certain regions of West Bengal & Bihar. These naxal outfits called for selective annihilation (only those who tormented the landless/poor) and economic blockade of the landed class. Since most of the dalits worked as manual workers on the farmlands of the land owning class, which was predominantly upper caste/powerful OBC, this agrarian struggle got divided on caste lines. The left wing extremism groups having solidarity for the landless, most of who belonged to the extremely backward/dalit castes, came to be regarded as the enemies of the landed class. The landed farmers formed their own armed outfits, the most notorious of which was the Ranvir Sena and thus, began a cycle of revenge and counter revenge between the naxals/their lower caste sympathizers and the private armies of landlords. The farming fields of Bihar converted into the killing fields.

After the mandalisation of polity in the 1990s, the powerful backward castes/intermediate castes began to wield enormous influence on the land assets in rural India. This transformation in the rural landscape of the country failed to provide any relief to the poor landless peasants and their fate remained unchanged. The exploitation cycle of the marginalized continued, only the configuration of the perpetrating class witnessed a slight change with the arrival of powerful backward castes in the landed group. The caste atrocities on dalits are related to the question of land possession in most parts of the country. At times, caste hatred gets mingled with caste oppression. Unlike north India where land was traditionally controlled by a small minority of Hindu upper castes/intermediate castes who never soiled their hands, the Jat Sikh peasantry of Punjab/Haryana took pride in working on their fields and was never a victim of the brahminical ideology of hatred for manual work. For these reasons, the relation between the Jat Sikh peasantry and the dalit agricultural labourers was not much mediated by as much as caste hatred as class oppression (economic exploitation). In the rural parts of north western India, caste based hatred and oppression were never of the scale as witnessed in northern India. However, this does not mean that the dominant Jat community did not use its privileged position for arm twisting local labour which often precipitated into the social boycott of dalits. The rural structure of the country and the plight of rural dalits are too important issues to be ignored by the proponents of the dalit movement who supposedly champion the dalit cause. Around 70 percent of the dalits reside in villages. Out of them, around three-fourth of the dalit households have either no land or are on the verge of landlessness. Most of the active male members of these families work as labourers on the fields of the farmers/landed class. It is a fact that even after more than 65 years of independence and despite the passing of acts prohibiting bonded labour and employment of children below the age of 14 in certain occupations by the union government; it is not uncommon to find bonded labourers and children below the age of 14 years employed on farmlands and elsewhere. Incidences of bonded labour may have come down but isn't it a blot on our democracy that it still exists and most of the victims are from the lower castes? Why only land owning castes; members of the money lending class should also be blamed for the plight of the dalits. In 2000, around 15-17 percent of the rural dalit households cultivated land. But for the lack of resources and lack of access to bank credit, they had to take loans from the local money lenders at exorbitant rates of interest. This resulted into a debt trap for them, threatening the very sources of their livelihood. The dalit workers employed on the fields lack the courage to speak against the big farmers/landlords for fear of being rendered jobless and often, they have to take the sides of their masters on any issue whether they like it or not. This lessens the scope for their autonomy and independence in decision making and thus is an affront on human dignity. It is a big blow to the aspirations of the lower castes. Remember the population of this marginalized class is substantial. The plight of the dalits in rural India can easily be conjectured by a few statistical highlights. According to NSS data (2003), 41.6 percent of the rural households did not have any land other than homesteads. The incidence of landlessness was higher among dalit households as around 56.5 percent of the dalit households did not own non homestead land. NSS data on ownership holdings show that in most of the states, the proportion of land owned by the scheduled caste households was very much lower than their share in the total population.

Take the case of the southern state of Tamil Nadu. In a recently highlighted case on NDTV (17/01/11), certain startling revelations were made. 20 lakh acres of land were given to the dalits under the panchammi scheme of the state. However, owing to illegal encroachments, sales and forceful evictions, dalits have been left with only 1 lakh hectares. Now, let's take a look at the reports of the National Campaign on Dalit Human Rights 2006. From 1948 to the 1970s, 349 million hectares of land were given to the farmers, out of which only 0.5 percent was given to the scheduled castes and tribes. The report also points out that out of an estimated 30 million hectares of harvestable surplus land, only 7.5 million hectares have been declared surplus and only a small portion of it has gone to the dalits.

Out of the total of 35 million hectares of land released as part of the ongoing land reform acts, less than 1 percent has gone to the depressed classes. The transfer of land as part of the state policy failed to reach them as they could not take possession of the government lands due to social dynamics and pressure from other social groups. It has become a common phenomenon to see dalit lands being usurped by the non dalits. This, often, is the bone of contention between the traditional power groups and the increasingly, assertive dalit groups.

The Green Revolution that took place in the country in the late 1960s subsidized agricultural production to a great extent but the impact was not widespread. It was limited to only a few select pockets of Punjab, Haryana, western UP and the Krishna Cauvery delta. Even in these areas, the major beneficiaries turned out to be the dominant powerful farming communities, possessing large farming tracts, not the landless dalits. The marginal farmers within the dalit communities could not afford tractors, irrigation facilities and the high yielding varieties of seeds. The revolution resulted in widening the already existing socio economic chasm between the dalits and the non dalits. The Cooperative movement that culminated in the establishment of agricultural cooperative societies to lend credit to agriculture and link production to the market helped the big farmers, most of who were of OBC/intermediate/upper castes. The dalits could never get their due.

Let's divert a little bit from the land problem and take into account another factor that has the potential to usher in far reaching transformation in rural India. 73rd Amendment Act of 1992 adding Part 1X to the constitution of India entitled "Panchayats" has been a wonderful chapter in the pages of Indian polity and is often described as the extension of our representative democracy from New Delhi to the doorsteps of rural India. The panchayats are entrusted with the task of planning and implementation of various socio economic welfare and development schemes at the village level. In the panchayat bodies to be filled up by direct elections, seats are to be reserved for scheduled castes in proportion to their total population. The seats of mukhiyas/sarpanchs were to be also reserved for scheduled castes in a prescribed ratio as determined by state legislatures to give them a sense of being decision makers in rural pockets of the country. **Though the functioning of our Panchayati raj institutions (PRI) has been far from satisfactory owing to lack of proper devolution of authority and finances from the state legislatures and local social dynamics, nevertheless, a beginning has already been made in the political decentralization process, after years of**

dithering. Panchayats have emerged as an important level within our federal structure, reservation at panchayat level is today a more important avenue of political participation for the dalits than within state or central legislatures. Dominance/power of a social group in rural India is generally associated with possession of land assets. Majority of the dalits living in villages are either landless or possess very little land. Traditionally, they had been dependent upon the rural elites to eke out a living and that living, too, came at the cost of their dignity. The rural elites had land and mostly belonged to the upper/powerful backward castes; they were moderately educated and had links with the state and the bureaucracy. It suited their interests to keep the lower castes in a degraded condition and that too, without voice. PRI and the public welfare programmes of the state have led to creation of opportunities for the lower castes to free themselves from the tentacles of the rural feudal elements and live on their own terms and conditions without compromising on their dignity. The recent PRI elections in some states witnessed several incidents of violence between rival communities. The lower caste people are now no longer ready to take things lying down and allow the dominant social groups to rig the polls and hence this cycle of violence and counter violence.

Unprecedented political mobilization of dalits has taken place, an identity has been constructed and now more and more dalits go to the polling booths to cast their votes. The extension of democracy to the grass root level has further deepened the process of political conscience in the dalits. The voting percentage of dalits has gone up and many dalit associations, organizations and parties have sprung up. The dalits are now more aware of their rights and their political awareness has increased by leaps and bounds. The traditional structure of rural dominance based on land and social status are undergoing change thanks to education, occupational diversification and government welfare and development programmes. New forms and manifestations of power have appeared which are in direct confrontation with the old ones, represented by the rural elites. The entire rural landscape is changing in values and ethos with frequent and increasing interactions with the urban areas. The power of the rural elites or to be precise, the rich farmers began to decline once the law of diminishing return set in agriculture and labour became expensive. The public investment and subsidies in agriculture witnessed a decline in percentage terms. Today, less than 15 percent of our Gross Domestic Product (GDP) is contributed by agriculture which still employs around 50 percent of our work force. On the contrast, compare it with the scenario in the early years after the attainment of independence. At that time, agriculture contributed to more than 50 percent of our GDP though the work force engaged in it was 80 percent. This is enough to show the extent of wastage of labour potential in the agro sector. A substantial percentage of rural folk moved to the towns and cities to get better job opportunities in the industry. Agriculture lost its pre eminence in the Indian economy and thus the reduction in the clout of communities dependent on it.

The change in situation is discernable but the desired acceleration seems to be not there. The rural social elites, now comprising of a good percentage of powerful backward caste communities, are not ready to digest the fact that the dalits are now occupying pivotal positions in PRI elected bodies. Hence, they resort to all sorts of machinations to remove the dalit representatives from those bodies by passing no confidence motions against them or creating hurdles in their path to prevent them from discharging their duties. During the time of local elections, muscle flexing is done by the dominant groups to intimidate the voters belonging to the lower caste communities and prevent them from contesting elections. In many instances, the local government bureaucracy tends to favour the privileged social groups. Mid day meal scheme, though run under the supervision of the panchayats in a fair number of states, face social boycott from the upper castes/intermediate backward castes when the meals are cooked by dalit women. This takes place in even those states which have dalit chief ministers. Upper/intermediate OBC caste people are yet not ready to let their children share meal with their fellow lower caste children. The dalit PRI functionaries do not seem to have the de facto power to implement panchayat schemes due to social hostility and rivalry. In various states, social welfare programmes like widow pensions, old age pensions, and awaas yojanas depend upon the identification of beneficiaries by the panchayats. Naturally, selection of beneficiaries is not based on the genuineness of cases but on local political power play. Dalits lose out in the process. Deserving poor dalit families are left out of BPL lists and have no access to ration cards. The socially dominant rural groups corner most of the benefits crowding out the marginalized groups in the process.

However, things are bound to change in the coming times. The days of traditional/primitive societies where social position is determined by caste or status are numbered. What we are witnessing today is that India is a transitional society where old social norms co exist with the new ones. The formalized institutions may be there but their working is very much of the primitive society type. The creation of democratic and equal society may see the proper social dynamics in the realm of Panchayati raj India. It's a well accepted fact that rural societies are more stratified and prone to caste based discriminations. If the institution of caste has to be weakened, the ground work for it must emanate from the rural countryside and for this to happen, it is imperative that the functioning of the PRI be made effective. PRI can make the greatest contribution in the realm of social revolution because it provides chances to the dalits to become decision makers in making policies that affect their daily lives. It provides them opportunities to engage with the powerful non dalit communities on an equal footing to discuss the problems affecting the socio economic development of their villages. Moreover, PRI provides the dalit movement with the option to develop a dedicated cadre of social activist dalit leaders, right at the lowest rung of our democratic edifice.

Coming back to the urban landscape, most of the urban dalits reside in areas that do not have the amenities, as seen in more developed and posh areas. The areas may be slums or semi slums where they are exposed to all types of vices like social crimes, petty thefts or drug addiction. The poorest sections among the urban dalits are compelled to live on pavements, traffic intersections or in vacant spaces/communal lands and eke out a living. Their dwelling places are dirty and filthy devoid of proper sanitation and hygiene factors. Most of them work in factories, construction sites and on pavements as petty hawkers. Very often, on the charges of unauthorized occupation of land or in the name of development, they are forcefully evicted from their habitations. Independent India and even the previous colonial regimes carried out huge developmental tasks like building big dams, setting up of public corporations, building roads/bridges/railway tracks/highways/flyovers, setting up of special economic zones etc. Most of the affected people belonged to the weak and vulnerable sections of the population, mostly the dalits and the adivasis. An estimated 30 million people had to leave their homes to make way for the carrying out of development work since 1950s but till now, a majority of them are languishing for want of proper compensation and rehabilitation. Indiscriminate development and increasing levels of urbanization have resulted in receding spaces for the poor, disadvantaged population who have virtually been driven to the state of despair. Tribal communities are losing their traditional forest rights, nursing grievances against the exploitative administrative machinery and this engendered frustration is driving them to swell the naxal ranks in several parts of eastern and central India. These communities live in acute economic conditions and can be easily lured by the Naxal leadership to become their foot soldiers. Recently, at Jantar Mantar in New Delhi, a few thousand representatives of various people's movements from all across the nation gathered to ventilate their grievances. They are the dalits, the tribals and sections of unprotected working class like farmers and the fishermen who all live by the land, forest and water bodies. They are up in arms against the state that wants to evict them, rob them of their meagre resources by transferring their resources to the corporate world on the ostensible plea of development without any adequate compensation and rehabilitation. They are protesting against the Land Acquisition, Rehabilitation and Settlement Bill. Prime urban and rural land is being acquired, while lakhs of hectares of barren wasteland are lying unattended. This policy has created ripples and is having wide ranging repercussions on rural countryside. In urban areas, bastis after bastis are being cleared of dwellers in the name of development, with windfall gains for the builders and the developers. There are genuine concerns of development which need land but underlying motive should be one of public purpose and not politico corporate greed. Moreover, any meaningful land acquisition must take the assent from majority of the stake holders and there has to be the adequacy of compensation and rehabilitation. The cost of the land to be given to the owners must be fair. Concerns related to ecology/environment must be addressed first before embarking on acquisition of land.

At present, a little over 46 percent of the country's area is cultivated. According to the Ministry of Agriculture reports, the net sown area declined by 1.5 percent between 1990-2003. While in percentage terms, this seems insignificant, in absolute terms, it translates to more than 21 lakh hectares. On the other hand, between 1994-2004, land under non agricultural use has gone up by 34 lakh hectares. This is a threat to our food security scenario. Besides, such a large scale diversion of agricultural land towards industry and repealing of land ceiling acts in several states, houses have become beyond the reach of even middle classes. This probably explains the proliferation of slums in most parts of urban India. According to latest NSSO figures, there are more than 33000 slum colonies in urban India at present, with Maharashtra topping the charts with more than 7000. Whether it is the Bhakra Nangal Project or the Narmada Dam or say, the Hirakud Project, coastal fishing communities, slum dwellers or victims of industrialization, each state has thousands of hapless people who have not been rehabilitated. The opportunity to democratize and decentralize planning to minimize diversion of land and destruction of agriculture and to stop uprooting people must be viewed with seriousness.

These issues call for remedial measures. As part of its agenda, it can present a charter of demands to the state like recognition of land rights for the dalits, protection of dalit lands from encroachment, recognition of their share in the common village properties, setting up of special courts to dispose land dispute cases involving dalits and stopping the eviction of dalits from their own lands in the name of development. These are the issues on which the dalit movement needs to spearhead a national agitation to make its voices heard by the ruling parties.

The discussion on dalits and land will not be complete until and unless, we divert our attention towards the new economic reforms and the forces of globalization/privatization that are shaping the contours of rural India. Till now, much of rural India has not been exposed to the liberalization bug but with the deepening of the reform process, changes in the structure of rural economy are bound to happen that can have repercussions for the rural sector. An increasing interaction with the current economic trends may result in the ultimate de peasantisation and corporatization of agriculture. The impact of reforms will, in all possibility, benefit the rich farmers who have large land holdings. The poor rural masses, most of who are landless and belong to the lower castes are likely to lose their sources of livelihood on the fields as introduction of mechanized technology driven agriculture might result in the curtailment of on farm job related opportunities. The leasing of agricultural lands and contract farming might change the very face of agricultural India as the focus will shift from the production of food crops to production of cash crops or in other words, market will decide what to produce and how to produce. According to Sainath, the per capita availability of food grains has declined every five years without exception from 1992 to 2010, whereas from 1972 to 1991, it has arisen every five years without exception. The average poor family in 1997 had about 100 kilograms more food grains than the average poor family in 2007. Farm incomes have collapsed. Hunger has grown very fast and at times, stray cases of starvation deaths have been reported from certain pockets of the country. Food grain stocks are rotting because of lack of proper food storage facilities. Even the Supreme Court has expressed dismay over the fact that how food grains can be allowed to rot in a country where millions go to sleep with a hungry stomach. Public investment in agriculture has declined appreciably. Employment has collapsed. Job opportunities have stagnated. Nothing has happened for the poor rural landless that has changed for the better.

The shift from basic cereals like rice, wheat, maize, pulses etc. to those that fetch remunerative prices in the market is likely to endanger the food security scenario in India. India's self sufficiency in food grain production will come to an end and the country will be forced to depend more and more on food grains import from outside. Add to it, the frequent fluctuations witnessed in the international food grains market and the adverse implications for India become more obvious. Just consider the scenario that is unfolding in the country at present. The prices of food grains are soaring at neck break speed and the government has been reduced to a mere spectator, content to look at helplessly at the exasperated poor and the middle classes. The decision making has shifted from the state and the farmers to the corporate. The corporatization of agriculture has induced mono culture i.e. sowing of one crop, large scale use of fertilizers/pesticides and the advent of genetically modified crops. This has created adverse consequences for ecology, depleting the intrinsic value of our natural resources like water and land. There is also the possibility of frequent occurrence of health hazards. All these are not going to affect the health of the corporate but definitely, the poor rural folk stand to lose out.

Rural economies across India have either stagnated, collapsed or are on the verge of collapsing since the advent of the 1990s. Small scale industry, the backstay of rural India, is stagnating. Artisans and craftsmen are becoming obsolete. The potters who used to make earthen vessels/toys and sell them at the time of village fairs have disappeared. The local bakeries, potato chip makers and the pickle makers have disappeared. Cottage industries are no match for the corporate. This slump in the fortunes of small industries makes the life of the poor all the more miserable.

What happened in the states of Maharashtra, Chattisgarh, Karnataka, Andhra Pradesh and the Madhya Pradesh? According to the National Crime Records Bureau, the total number of farmer suicides since 1995 stands at around 2.75 lakhs. The figure for Maharashtra, alone, stands at 54000. During the time, public investment in agriculture shrunk to a mere 2 percent of the GDP. What may be the possible reason for this wave of farmer suicides, affecting a good part of the country? A fear of hopelessness, among the farmers, most of whom were at the subsistence level or marginal, near marginal levels, failed crops in the drought season, lack of on farm and off farm works and lack of adequate state social assistance/social security measures. Their misery was compounded by the fact that most of them were caught in a debt trap with no possible chances of repayment of loans. The introduction of BT cotton and other genetically modified crops also made the farmers depended on the multinationals for the supply of seeds which were not renewable thus increasing the cost of production.

Most of the victims of the agrarian crisis belonged to the landless and the poor, a fair percentage of who belonged to the scheduled castes and extremely backward communities. The politicians, including the dalit leaders, are content paying lip service to their woes. The dalit leaders/intelligentsia look the other way because they feel that this problem is not theirs.

This problem has no connection with reservation or Ambedkar, so why should they bother? This problem is not linked to the interests of the neo empowered or the elite dalit class and is basically concerned with the rural starving dalit masses; so, why should they be worried? It is not that no one is aware of the reasons of drought that has left large tracts of Maharashtra distressed. The recurring drought has got more to do with lack of proper water management than failure of monsoon. The water, meant for irrigation, was diverted towards industry especially the big sugar mills that are controlled by high profile Maratha leadership. The dalit leaders won't say anything on this because this would hamper their chances of electoral understanding.

Dalit Movement: A victim of symbolism & patronage politics

A lot of hue and cry has been raised over the construction of the statues of dalit icons, elephants, Ambedkar parks and the Dalit Prerna Sthal in Noida in western Uttar Pradesh by the erstwhile Bahujan Samaj Party. The rapid indiscriminate construction spree has invited wrath of the non dalits and the opposition parties who have accused the dalit leader Mayawati of indulging in cheap political gimmick in furtherance of her political agenda. Criticisms have ranged from damage to ecology to sheer splurging & wastage of public money on constructions that are not going to produce any material benefits for the oppressed or result in any sort of social revolution. Corruption charges have been levelled against top BSP functionaries and pliant bureaucrats. Already there are talks in Samajwadi circles of the need to utilize the vacant spaces of Ambedkar parks for the purposes of education and community functions. Now let us contemplate to get to the crux of the matter; why this brouhaha over acts of dalit symbolism? After all symbols have played a major role in conveying both social and political messages. Mahatma Gandhi had undertaken the famous civil disobedience movement by making salt the symbol of protest. The Mahatma knew the significance of salt as a common daily household consumption item. When Nelson Mandela talked of reconciliation between the blacks and the whites, he followed it up by turning up for an international rugby match as a symbol of reaching out to the whites. It is pertinent to point out that until then; rugby was regarded as a white man's game in South Africa.

For centuries the dalits were subjugated and humiliated in a highly differentiated and exploitative social structure where caste determined the position in social hierarchy. After independence, the socio economic position of the dalits improved to some extent; their representation may have increased in public employment and legislatures but the stigma attached at being born in a low caste remained and continues to haunt them from time to time. The non dalit perceptions towards them have not yet changed and even today, they are regarded as the ones who have no merits and thrive on state dole outs/charity. However the deepening of the social democratic process and the concomitant surfacing of identity politics have enabled the dalit movement to make its presence felt in the socio political life of the nation. The oppressed want to have a voice, present their own alternate views about state, culture & political philosophy and nothing can be better than display of radical progressive dalit symbols and imposition of the statues of dalit icons at public places, in order to develop an understanding of dalit aspirations & history among the general public. The installation of these monuments, along with renaming certain districts after the names of the dalit icons, has instilled a sense of pride and self respect in the overall dalit population in UP. The dalits are finally celebrating their achievements.

Naturally the social elites are not impressed by this assertive growing democratic consciousness of the dalits. Alternative symbolism propounded by the dalit movement is drastically different from the value system, political thoughts and yardsticks of so called secular public symbols of the elites, most of who are either upper castes or intermediate backward castes. The elites are feeling offended as until now, they thought it was their prerogative to construct national symbols and claim for their universal acceptance. They feel that this alternate dalit symbolism is sheer blasphemy and an encroachment upon their socio political territory. However they need to do some soul searching and accept the fact that dalits have as much stake in democracy as themselves and hence their genuine participation in the democratization of public spaces need not raise their hackles. The contemporary Indian socio political landscape is crisscrossed by intense democratic competition between a plethora of stake holders, read castes/communities/religions, with each of them determined to revisit history through a prism of multiple ideology, claims and aims. The subaltern groups like dalits are now no longer hesitant to challenge the dominant socio cultural hegemony of the social elites by their own symbolic interpretations and decoding. The symbols or the dalit monuments may be ridiculed by the non dalits but for the dalits, they have immense value. They are widely perceived to be the fulcrum of equality and democracy, the core of the rising aspirations & democratic consciousness of the dalits and the assertion of the fact that the dalit movement has finally come of age.

Huge amount of expenditure incurred by the dalit leadership in UP may have raised the eyebrows of the non dalit masses but as far as the common dalit masses are concerned, they are applauding because till now, they were used to seeing statues of upper caste leaders at public places with whom they could not identify themselves. The fact that their fellow brethren are getting idolized is a matter of joy for them; the fact that their viewpoints and thoughts are finding space in our democracy is a matter of celebration for them. **Mayawati's political stock may have come down in the eyes of the non dalits for her extravagant expenditure of public money on dalit idols but make no mistake about it; the importance of the dalit tsarina has gone up among the deprived classes as for the first time, they are witnessing a dalit leader who is not afraid to take on the upper castes and is ready to pay them back in the same coin. She is ready to send the message to the upper caste leadership that if they can construct their statues, why not she?** The statues will certainly give the dalits a sense of history and hundreds of years later, when the common dalits will see the statues of Ambedkar, Periyar and Mayawati, their chests will simply swell with pride.

What the dalit leadership did in UP is not something new to Indian political firmament. It simply tried to emulate the cult worshipping trend of the Congress party which installed innumerable statues of Mahatma Gandhi, members belonging to the Nehru-Gandhi family and other great leaders of the party. However, the Congress did it at a time when it enjoyed wide support among all the cross sections of the population. There was no alternative political party which could challenge the supremacy of the party. To cap it all, the Congress was synonymous with the freedom struggle against the colonial and the imperial British power. Democracy was at its nascent stage and the political mobilization process, centered on community/caste/religion had not taken off in a great way and this enabled the Congress to get away with it. But now, universal adult franchise has deepened our democracy, the social dynamics are changing fast and the interplay of various centrifugal forces are threatening to tear apart the unified social fabric of the nation. In the current political scenario of a fractured nature where caste/identity affiliations are the defining features, any brand of politics based on identity/ symbolism is bound to bring it into conflict with competing identity/ideology. This is what is currently happening in UP where a resurgent Samajwadi Party is contemplating to counter the iconic Ambedkar with the leading socialist ideologue Ram Manohar Lohia. The dalit symbols are challenged by the installation of the statues of great socialist leaders like Lohia, Karpoori Thakur and of course, the redoubtable JP Narayan.

This, sort of problem, gets accentuated when we are confronted with a multitude of communities, castes and religions that inhabit our nation and each of them starts its naked assertion of symbolism. There is the danger of national identity being submerged and the caste/religious/ethnic/regional/linguistic identities taking precedence. Moreover blatant display of identity/symbolism by the dalit leadership might lead to other social groups becoming antagonistic to the dalit movement. This might cut at the very roots of the expansion programme of the dalit parties. The dalit intelligentsia may bask in the glory of the cultural assertion of the dalits but politically, the results will be nothing sort of a disaster for the movement as the dalits haven't yet achieved the critical mass to alter the course of Indian polity on their own.

Mayawati's symbolism did not go down well with the non dalits and this, perhaps, is one of the reasons for the BSP's dismal electoral performance in the 2012 Assembly Elections in UP. It was widely believed that huge amount of tax payers' money was unnecessarily splurged on the building of statues and parks and that, too, in a state where the quality of life of a common man is not very encouraging. Several corruption charges have also come up against the Government in the construction of dalit monuments. Now, even the statues of dalit icons that were built were mostly of those who belonged to the powerful and dominant castes within the dalit community while the numerically or electorally less significant ones were left out of the process and forgotten. It is very difficult to surmise whether the statues had a mobilizing or de mobilizing impact on the dalits but the symbols failed to bring the BSP to power once again or provide tangible benefits to the downtrodden. The problem with symbolism is that it may resonate with the poor and the illiterate but not with the educated, well off middle class dalits. The well off dalit sections are more concerned with issues related to their upward mobility, development and governance. Despite belonging to the lower castes, they identify themselves with the class interests of the middle class population after attaining adequate socio economic development.

Patronage politics is what most of the political parties are adept at, in practising in India. The spoils of power are shared among the party members. The parties generally implement the welfare or development programmes that are tailor made for their constituencies. The situation has exacerbated with the emergence of powerful regional parties in most of the electorally important states of the Indian union. These regional parties are mostly based on caste, community, religion and other identity factors. For them, their constituency matters more than the overall population. Since they do not have a national perspective or an economic insight, they depend on extension of patronage to their respective constituencies to increase their support base or keep themselves politically relevant. This is not to absolve the mainstream national parties of the charges of patronage politics but the charges against them can't be easily substantiated.

Mayawati's Ambedkar Gram Vikas Yojana was intended to develop model villages but this Yojana was applicable to only those villages which had a fair percentage of scheduled castes. Similarly, Kanshiram Sahari Vikas Yojana was intended to help the weaker sections build their modest accommodation in the towns. Mahamaya Yojana, though professing to alleviate the poverty of people belonging to all communities, was in fact, tilted towards the dalits because the selection of the beneficiaries was done on a points system, the dalits given advantage in this system, on account of their caste. These schemes may have appeal among the deprived dalit population but when it comes to the educated, well off sections of the dalit population, the politics of patronage simply refuses to convert into votes. The aspirations of the upwardly mobile dalits have gone up and they are no longer content to accept dole outs and largesse from the dalit leadership or the state. They aspire for higher goals and want empowerment and participation in development rather than accept the tag of being passive beneficiaries. It's high time for the dalit leadership to step out of the parameters of symbolism and patronage politics and concentrate on broader issues related to development and governance.

The demand for erection of statues is not something new to Indian politics. Way back in the early fifties, there was a clamour for installation of statues of different leaders but there were perils involved in the process. Nehru's modernism probably made him wary of personality cults and it is likely that this may be the reason why no central policy was initiated in the 1950s to fund statues in the country. For a modernist liberal like Nehru, apotheosisation of an individual was not proper. He felt that the statues have historically been built of gods/goddesses in our country and not human beings.

The Indian freedom movement was not a homogenous movement; it carried along with it divergent socio political streams of opinion and hence, a plethora of icons having distinct ideologies/opinions emerged on the national scale. It was indeed a Hobson's choice to construct a statue of one, leaving out the other. The socialist stalwarts were apprehensive of the cult status of Nehru and his family. For Ambedkar, hero worship or say, erection of statues was a sure way to the degeneration of democracy. The Congress built statues of its leaders despite Nehru's apathy towards cult worship. Today symbols are more a matter of political expediency than faith. Leaders of today, including the dalit leadership, are so much blinded by a sense of parochial identity that for them, vote bank politics matter more than the ideology of that very icon whose statue they are building.

High population pressure and the demands of unbridled industrialization-urbanization are taking their toll on the scarce land spaces, the land for common public usage is shrinking and yet in the name of icons, huge tracts of land are being set aside without being put to use for public purpose. The statues, monuments, parks and samadhis are occupying a fair percentage of our prime land and with the kind of identity politics that is played out in democratic India; the increasing iconisation of our scarce land resources may deprive millions of Indians from having public spaces and affordable housing facilities.

New Economic Reforms and dalit movement

The crisis driven economic reforms, which began in the early nineties, were based on the assumption that though hardships for common people would occur in the initial years, the trickle down phenomenon later onwards will make sure that the fruits of economic development would percolate down to the lowest strata of the society. More than twenty years have elapsed since the onset of the reform process but what we have witnessed is the rather skewed distribution of the benefits of globalization. More than three fourth of the population still continues to be left out of the reform process. Barring a few aberrations, our GDP has grown at an appreciable rate but this phenomenon has not been translated into improved human development indices or a better quality of life for the teeming masses. It is pointed out that there has been a net increase of wealth, close to US $ 1 trillion in the Indian stock market in the time frame of 2003-2007, where only 5 percent of our population has equity. According to the World Bank, around 42 percent population of India lives below the poverty line i.e. spends less than $ 1.25 per day. 212 women still die, out of 1 lakh, due to the lack of medical facilities. More than 40 percent of the children suffer from mal nutrition resulting in stunted growth. A hub of economic activity centre like Mumbai is home to around 50 percent of its population residing in slums/semi slums. On the other hand, contours of a new emerging India is also visible with galloping urbanization, more BMWs plying on roads, more luxury shopping malls, sprouting of industrial hubs and a boom in real estate. The new economic reforms have led to the creation of vast economic inequalities with the rich getting richer and the poor getting poorer.

Now let us come to the original topic of our discussion. How have the reforms affected the dalits? Has the New Economic Programme (NEP) led to their genuine empowerment or has it been a chimera to them? Why do the leaders of the dalit movement view NEP with suspicion?

After the dismantling of the license, quota, permit raj—the focus shifted to LPG (Liberalization, Privatization and Globalization) in 1991. Easing out of restrictions to facilitate trade, simplification of investment rules, restructuring of the capital market, withdrawal of the state from many sectors and the entry of the private players created the ground for the launch of NEP thereby signaling a departure from the Nehruvian legacy of socialism and state control of economic activities. **The retreat of the state was like a bolt from the blue for the scheduled castes as even today, for many dalits; state is synonymous with the constitution, the same constitution which was given to the state by the iconic Ambedkar.** The welfare nature of the state provided constitutional safeguards to protect the dalit interests and also made positive affirmative action plans for furthering their cause and empowerment. No one can dispute the fact that the policy of reservation as part of the conscious state policy enabled the dalits to make their presence felt in public employment and the legislatures. It is the common refrain of the dalit movement that the ethos of free market can't be juxtaposed with positive discrimination in favour of the marginalized communities and with the democratic spirit of the constitution. **The very nature of the Indian state with its emphasis on equality and social justice is not congruent with the market imperatives of LPG whose sole preoccupations are with merit, competition and efficiency.**

Post independence, the state implemented reservation for dalits in public employment, legislatures and local bodies. This was the prime driving force behind increasing the representation of dalits in central and state government departments, public corporations and other bodies receiving state aid. The increased employment opportunities of the dalits led to their increased visibility and assimilation into the social mainstream and at the same time, created hopes in the minds of millions for a better living and more social recognition. However, the advent of NEP led to structural changes in the economy like entry of private players, strategic partnerships between the public and private firms resulting in joint ventures, arrival of multinational companies transcending national boundaries and the gradual retreat of the state from many sectors of the economy with the concomitant downsizing of bureaucracy and disinvestment in profit making public sector utilities. This affected the dalit interests adversely as the private firms, multinationals and the joint ventures with diluted governmental share holding were not under any constitutional obligation to fix a certain percentage of seats for the dalits. The age old prejudice against the dalits, coupled with increasing stress on efficiency and competition led to their dwindling employment opportunities. Downsizing of the government resulted in a loss of state jobs also as the motto of NEP became lean, thin and mean government. New Public Management dictated adherence to state minimalism. The days of permanent government jobs have become numbered and new job concepts like contract employment, casual temporary jobs based on needs and outsourcing are doing the rounds. The age old security related with government jobs is now fast becoming a thing of the past. The market forces are solely concerned with profit motives and can't be expected to function as the agents of social transformation as opposed to the philosophy of the state and hence the dalits are feeling let down in this fast changing world. Dalit class generally worked as artisans and lacked an entrepreunal culture. Age old prejudices/discrimination/hostility towards them led them to taking less to professions. The dalit war cry of reservation in the private sector is just like the old wine in the new bottle. Whether this demand is going to be met or not, it is difficult to say.

Today's world economic order is held hostage to a new form of capitalism that is commonly referred to as finance capitalism. We have witnessed the power of finance capitalism as the global economy plummeted into turmoil in 2008 and 2011-12. Sovereign states have been compelled to bail out the huge corporations by giving them the tax payers' money; matters do not end at this and policy making, the prerogative of the sovereign state has been so tailored so as to reflect the concerns of the big players and corporate. The establishment of World Trade Organization and the international financial architecture like the Asian Development Bank and the World Bank have laid down rules of international trade that are to be followed by the member countries. In this age of global connect; it is very cumbersome for any nation to impose its unilateral agenda on the non state player.

The corporate, instead of acceding to the principle of reservation in the private sector, may view the intention of the government with hostility. Unlike the state, the ultimate objective of the private sector is profit maximization; the sense of social responsibility or social agenda is yet to see its evolution there. Rather than raising the pitch for reservation in private sector and dividing the society, the dalit movement has to make extra efforts for alternatives. It has to introspect whether the dalit masses, not the privileged dalit elites, are ready to swim with the tide of globalization. Are the dalit masses ready to take the bull by the horns? Global industry and highly specialized services require highly skilled and trained man power to handle the job descriptions of the neo global order. For this, the global industry needs personnel who are well equipped with higher education in the fields of management, information technology, bio technology, engineering and other disciplines. Most of the dalits who work in urban areas and rural areas do not possess the technical requisites commensurate with the global job profiles. Naturally, the job markets are not favourable to them. Hence, the first motive of the dalit movement should be to direct their energies towards securing quality education for the dalit youth. There should be emphasis on skill development by incorporation of programmes like apprenticeship training and vocational training.

More and more dalit youths should be encouraged to take up medical, engineering and management education. The government should direct the banks to provide loans to the needy lower caste students on a priority basis. Industry can be given incentives by the state to impart skill development training programmes for the dalit youths.

Moreover the social responsibility clause has to be inserted while giving permission for the opening of industries/giving land on the part of the government. The focus of the movement should shift away from crying hoarse demanding reservation in private sector and instead, be directed at influencing the state policy in such a way so as to provide maximum opportunities for the higher education of the dalits in a big way as this will help them in standing up the challenges thrown at them by the deepening globalization process. We have already witnessed the neo dalit elite class, who had been the beneficiaries of reservation for one or more than one generation take advantage of the NEP and climb up the social ladder. A new dalit generation has arisen for whom private sector offers new opportunities for which they are well equipped backed up by better education. The entry of foreign universities in a big way is also likely to result in sweeping changes in the education sector. Today, educational institutions in the country, even autonomous ones like the IITs and the IIMs provide assistance scholarships to the needy SC/ST students apart from reserving a certain percentage of seats for them, but now, with the coming in of foreign/private universities and the increasing corporatization of education sector, will this be a reality? This is a multibillion dollar question baffling the minds of dalit youth but has the dalit movement given a serious thought to it? The new economic reform process has led to the mushrooming of a lot of engineering and management colleges and setting up of private universities who are solely guided by the rules of commercialization. Most of them are backed by politicians and corporate and charge hefty capitation fees from the students. How many dalits, barring the elite ones among them, are in a position to afford such a costly education for their children? For them, state run universities offer the only hope but with immense competition engendered with the arrival of resource rich foreign universities, will the state universities be in a position to withstand their onslaught?

Why higher education and colleges? Let's start from the primary education. The students of the Convent English Medium schools, most of who belong to the upper castes, the intermediate or the elite dalit class are in an advantageous position right from the beginning, in comparisons to the vernacular government primary schools which teach majority of the children belonging to the dalit/extremely backward class. For them, even primary education is a luxury which their parents can't afford. Mid day meals in these schools may have increased the level of enrollment and led to a decrease in the percentage of school drop outs as the screaming govt. records point out but has it bettered the quality of education or in other words, has it brought the rural dalit students on the same pedestal as the convent students of the privileged class? Why reservation? Why not heal them completely? Why has the dalit leadership not thought of advocating for uniformity in initial education and the adoption of a uniform school curriculum? Why this differential educational segregation?

The present day capitalism model treats the Govt's commitment to social obligations and poverty alleviation programmes as unproductive expenditure. The World bank—IMF duo, in the name of structural adjustment programme, supports the pruning down of subsidies/state expenditure with the logic of reducing the fiscal deficit so as to make the economy competitive and growth oriented. After the global economic crisis of 2008 and 2011-12, the entire Euro zone was in a mess. The USA after showing signs of an economic slowdown, is slowly trying to limp back to the path of economic recovery. European countries like Greece, Spain, Italy and France have been hit hard by the austerity bug. Popularly elected heads of state in Italy and Greece have been forced to abdicate in favour of technocrats/bankers at the diktats of finance capitalism. The world is increasingly moving towards a very dangerous phase of history where the forces of neo capitalism are threatening to sabotage the very essence of democracy. The democratically elected leaders are not making policies designed to help the masses; their hands in policy making are tied and influenced by the demands and concerns of big corporations and finance capital. Developed world is home to mass public protests due to rising levels of unemployment among the youth, cuts in government expenditure on education/healthcare and a near dismantling of the social assistance/social security apparatus. India can't afford to live in the fool's paradise. In our country too, outlays on health and education have not increased in the desired ratios. Our expenditure on education continues to be a little over 3 percent of our GDP, approximately the same as that of the 1990s level. Total expenditure in the healthcare sector is less than 2 percent of our GDP. Sectoral component plans targeting scheduled caste/tribal population have either decreased in size or have not increased to the desired ratios, resulting in increased levels of deprivation among them. State subsidies to the vulnerable groups are being pruned in the name of reduction of fiscal deficit. All these measures are leading to less public spending on a vast majority of the population. The dalits and the extremely backward castes, being at the base of development pyramid are the most affected.

Take for example—the MNERGA. This nationwide scheme, guaranteeing a minimum of 100 working days to a person of a household willing to work, at a minimum ceiling wage, was launched by the UPA 1 government in 2006. Despite a lot of loopholes and charges of rampant corruption in the implementation of the scheme, no one can deny the fact that MNREGA is slowly but steadily changing the face of rural India. The landless peasants & the marginal farmers, most of who belong to the dalit and the extremely backward castes, do not have to depend on the upper/intermediate/powerful backward caste farmers for on farm or off farm work opportunities. They can easily find employment opportunities in public works under this scheme like digging of ponds, digging canals, building village roads etc. They are assured of a minimum fixed daily wage while earlier; they were made to work by the socially dominant, powerful farmers at very low rates of wages and often under sub human conditions. Their dignity has now been restored by MNREGA and don't be surprised if now, you find these once mute faces developing an independent line of thinking from their erstwhile employers and voting independently and differently from the landed peasantry. In fact, MNREGA has become the bone of contention between political parties reflecting the fault lines in the interests of their core constituencies. Some powerful OBC dominated parties championing the cause of dominant farming communities feel that the scheme has led to a drop in agricultural production as the farmers are not assured of adequate labour supply and the labour costs have simply rocketed. Some economists argue that MNREGA has been a huge drag on the meagre economic resources of the state that is threatening the sustainability of our economy. Whatever, the opinion may be, the fact remains that MNREGA has empowered the lower castes, increased their income levels and autonomy in decision making. Govt of India's ambitious Food Security Legislation i.e. National Food Security Act based on entitlement of food grains to 75 percent population of the rural population and 50 percent of the urban population at heavily subsidized prices has been marred by protests from several quarters who feel that such huge state expenditure may increase our fiscal deficit. Some political parties, under pressure from the powerful farming community lobby, accuse the bill of being anti farmer as the farmers may not get remunerative prices for their products. The capitalist voices have blamed the state of doling out largess to the poor at the expense of pockets of the tax payers. These capitalists and corporate very well forget the huge concessions given to them in the form of tax holidays, cheap land and cheap electricity. This scheme will be immensely beneficial for improving the rampant mal nutrition and food deprivation levels of millions of poor people. No doubt, with the state of our Public Distribution System in shambles, the identification of beneficiaries a tough proposition and lack of a strong storage network, the implementation of this Act may lead to problems but then, it is a gamble worth taking.

These social intervention programmes are under attack today in the neo liberal economic set up. The states are being coerced into adopting austerity measures and cut down on their social obligations to reduce their burgeoning deficits. The social obligations are being regarded as largely unproductive expenditure which does not lead to either creation of durable assets or increased investment inflows. A fair section of our society is cynical towards pro people governmental programmes like Universal Educational Scheme and National Rural Health Mission or take National Urban Renewable plan or National Social Assistance plan. All these schemes are being termed populist that are increasing our fiscal concerns.

The past two decades have seen the Indian economy growing at a good pace, barring some aberrations but that improved GDP growth rate has not resulted into better human development indicators for the entire nation. Public investment in crucial sectors like education, health and agriculture has not kept pace with the needs. A vast majority of our population is untouched from the benefits of the NEP and with the tendency of the state to cut down on public investment in social sector involving those, things are not looking any brighter for them. For such segment of our population, state offers the only hope and that hope expects social security/assistance legislations from the state. The democratic system of our nation simply can't sustain if it fails to address the concerns of the vast majority. A middle ground needs to be found between the concerns of the industry and the welfare obligations of the state. Obsession with investment inflows and stock markets are understandable but that should not be at the cost of deprivation of the majority.

The international global finance order, today, is heavily biased towards neo forms of predatory capitalism. Giving food rights, land rights, limited employment rights and education rights to the vulnerable sections of our population like the dalits, tribals and the extremely backward castes and that, too, by incurring huge state costs is not regarded as pro growth. The capitalists hold state social assistance/ security schemes as unproductive expenditure which might lead to burgeoning fiscal deficits and might not be sustainable for our economy. Yes, foreign investment is desirable to give impetus to the growth of the economy but that does not mean that all our policies should be designed to further the interests of the private capitalism. The state does have an obligation towards the weak and vulnerable sections. Growth is desirable, investment is welcome but the benefits have to spread over the entire population. The European countries first became industrialized and generated wealth before adopting the path of democracy, universal adult suffrage and distributive policies to promote equality. India became democratic with universal adult voting rights without even having a modicum of economic development and the focus shifted to clamour for distribution of resources, which were not yet created.

Most of the capitalist European countries have put in place sound universal health schemes, universal social security schemes and educational assistance schemes to enable their population to absorb the shocks engendered by capitalism. Several Asian countries and China invested heavily in health, education and land reforms before embarking on capitalism. India has leapfrogged all stages and jumped on the LPG bandwagon without improving the quality of life of its citizens or having a proper social safeguard mechanism for the working class or its deprived citizenry. Government social security schemes are a necessity both factually and politically. The politicians have to keep an eye on the needs of their constituency which may want direct benefits in lieu of their votes. The dalit movement or the dalit leadership must be aware of the fact that these schemes are more productive for the vulnerable dalit sections as the majority dalit population tends to benefit from these. The universal social assistance schemes may not have much appeal for the dalit intelligentsia/leadership but the fact remains that these schemes have more potential to bring about a change in the quality of their lives in comparison to reservation.

The Indian growth story, starting from 2003 onwards has been made possible by large inflows of foreign capital which has largely gone into debt finance instruments, without in any way contributing to the increase in real income for the people. The volatile nature of the capital inflows is a cause for greater concern as has been witnessed in the East Asian crisis of 1997. According to the noted economist, Amartya Sen, the real growth of a nation is not measured in terms of GDP growth rate, but by the changes in the real income levels of the commoners, growth in employment, reduction in the level of socio economic inequality and improved human development indices in education and healthcare. The remarkable strides made by the East Asian economies and Japan was made possible after huge investments in the social sector by the state. Improved human development indices have always preceded the economic growth in most of the countries. The anomaly in India is evident. The policy makers want more growth but are hardly concerned about low performance in social sector, especially in education and health. Moreover, the focus of growth has shifted from production/manufacture to finance/stock markets and of course, speculative trading. The India Shinning Campaign of the NDA failed to translate into votes as the high growth rate of the Indian economy failed to percolate down to the masses, resulting in increased deprivation levels among them. The Indian growth story was not based on sound economic fundamentals as agriculture continued to be in distress and industrial growth, particularly in the manufacturing sector, was not commensurate with the requirements. Stock market boom was no consolation for the millions of our impoverished masses because it was only for 5-8 percent of our population and hence, was not indicative of the general welfare level of the population. The impetus provided by the services sector contributed maximum to our GDP growth while the performance of our manufacturing sector hit the rock bottom. A country like China managed to insulate its economy from the global economic turmoil in 2008 and 2011-12, thanks to its strong manufacturing sector performance. The ongoing world financial crisis, unlike in 2008, is already having a contagion effect on India. The rupee is devaluating sharply, the current account deficit is becoming unsustainable at 4.5 percent of our GDP, forex reserves are dwindling and the inflation is galloping at a neck break speed. The real income levels of the people are being squeezed resulting in contraction of demand which certainly is not a good sign for industry and overall growth of the industry. To tide over this, the government has to go for reduced public spending and cuts in subsidies which again results in hardship to common man.

The international financial credit rating agencies have already begun to downgrade India and the country's image as a favourable investment destination has taken a beating. The government is being lambasted for going slow on second generation reforms and being plagued by policy paralysis. The fleeing of foreign capital due to loss of the confidence of the investors is also a cause of major concern. Heavy oil import bill has led to serious imbalances in trade. The soaring prices of food grains and other items of daily consumption have left the common man groaning in pain. The national savings have also come down. An air of pessimism exists. The decision of the government to go for FDI in retail despite vociferous protests from the opposition was directed at restoring the confidence of the investors and generate some resources. The proposals for FDI in insurance and pensions are in the House. FDI in retail has the potential to endanger the source of livelihood of thousands of small, petty traders, the shopkeepers and the vegetable/fruit vendors. FDI in pension funds and insurance will expose the common man to the influence of the market forces which have different motives which may not be pro people. The government of the day, probably, has more faith in the ranking of the credit rating agencies than in the discharge of its constitutional obligations. It is not rare to see the international credit rating agencies furthering the cause of finance capital, rather than doing their works honestly. It does not behove the political leadership of the world's largest democracy to lose sleep over the forecasts/analysis of the credit rating agencies whose credibility does not inspire much confidence. The fault lies in us, in the way we have managed our macroeconomic policies. The capitalist class could not properly utilize the investment inflows which mostly went into unproductive activities and in course of time, turned into debts. The politico corporate nexus in the loot of scarce natural resources like spectrum, coal, iron ore, land etc also created complications for economy.

India has been traditionally a labour intensive economy. Introduction of labour saving devices/ technology has already reduced the job opportunities. The NEP has created openings for highly skilled employees. The rural population that is migrating to the urban areas in search of greener pastures is at a loss and feels frustrated as they do not have the educational qualification/expertise to take up the kind of jobs that are proliferating due to NEP. Around 80 percent of our work force in the informal sector is out of the radar screen of liberalization. These workers are not properly paid and are compelled to work for long hours. Their salaries have not kept pace with the increase in the cost of living while on the other hand; the software/skilled personnel are making a lot of fast money. The informal sector workers are never sure whether they will remain in their jobs or will be kicked out and to compound their woes, the state social assistance programme is not forthcoming. The inflation upward spiral has already reduced their real incomes and lowered their quality of life.

The dalit movement should take note of these happenings. Though these problems affect the entire working class, the vulnerable sections of the society are feeling more heat. The dalit interest is not at logger heads with the common interests as globalization does not make a distinction between a dalit and a non dalit. The dalit leadership must strive to make common ends with other segments of the population that is suffering due to NEP. Most of the dalits and the extreme backwards that are flocking to the urban corridors are forced to take up manual/unskilled work like doing the work of cleaners in hotels/restaurants, security guards at various installations, carrying bricks at construction sites etc. They do not possess the requisite criteria to do quality work in the formal sector. Most of them find habitations in urban slums or other vacant urban spaces devoid of proper hygiene and sanitary conditions. The children of these hapless human beings are deprived of education and fall prey to social crimes like theft, prostitution and drug addiction. Since most of them are migrants coming from the less developed parts of the country, they often are victims of discrimination at work places. They find problems in establishing their identity, lack documents like voter cards, ration cards etc. and hence, do not have access to the various forms of state social assistance/social security programmes. Has any top notch dalit leader or an eminent dalit intellectual shed any light on their plight? Has the dalit movement expressed any genuine concern for them that is reflected in its deed or agenda?

One of the features of LPG has been the indiscriminate land acquisitions by the private companies for the development of shopping malls, residential complexes, special economic zones and the industries. What does the state do? In the pre liberalization era, whatever may have been the shortfalls in governance, the state always appeared to be the protector of interests of the disadvantaged and the working class. Being pro capitalist was perceived to be a trait that was not in consonance with the ethos and welfare orientation of the constitution. However, once the LPG phase commenced, the New Public Management (NPM) theorists began to harp on the need of the state to opt for minimalism and retreat from the sphere of economic activities, barring a few sectors related to defense and state security. The common refrain of the NPM was that the government should act as facilitators and regulators of activities rather than doers. In the garb of NPM, the neo liberal phase grew wings and most of the governments worldwide colluded with the corporate in the plunder of natural resources. The interests of the commoners/working class became secondary and they were left on their own to fend for themselves. India was not immune to the developments taking place around the globe. We witnessed the trend in Singur/Nandigram in West Bengal when the ruling party cadre indulged in violence against the people agitating for their land rights.

Then we saw the plight of the Vedanta project in eastern state of Orissa. Not only is the matter related to land acquisition but there are also problems of environmental degradation/pollution. The commissioning of the Kudankulum nuclear plant in Tamil Nadu led to skirmishes between the government and the local fishing communities, most of whom were apprehensive of the safety measures of the plant and the likely impact on the aquatic environment. Instead of assuaging them and allaying their fears, the state took to police measures to suppress their movement. In the absence of any foolproof land acquisition act, the private companies, backed by colluding, acquiescing administrative machinery, contemplate to snatch away land from its legal owners.

Lakhs of acres of fertile agricultural tracts are being diverted for the purpose of industry and residential complexes. In the agricultural lands, even the trends of crop production are changing, with more focus on cash crops than food crops, posing a serious threat to our food security scenario. The declining agricultural lands have reduced on farm job opportunities for the poor landless rural folk. Urban sprawls are spreading at a fast pace, with the phenomenon being more conspicuous around the growth poles i.e. industrial centres. Mumbai-Pune corridor, Kolkata-Burdwan-Asansol corridor, Amhedabad-Baroda-Surat corridor, Delhi-Noida-Gurgaon-Faridabad corridor etc. are industrializing rapidly leading to large scale acquisitions of land from the rural hinterlands. The land owners/ big farmers are getting good prices for their lands. Here also, most of the dalits are left out of the race as they possess very little land or are virtually landless.

We can't opine that the LPG phase has only harmed the dalit interests; rather it has proved to be a blessing in disguise to some extent as the fast paced urbanization process threatens to break the age old shackles of caste based discriminations. Ambedkar felt that the traditional Indian rural society was based on brahminical social order in which the lower caste people were subjected to humiliation. He had exhorted his followers to move towards the towns and cities as the colonial factories located there would provide them livelihood while at the same time, facilitating their freedom from caste bondage system of rural India. The traditional occupational structure based on caste is missing in urban life, thus providing an opportunity to the dalit youths to take up employment according to their predilections and not, according to the caste in which they are born. It is pertinent to point out that Mahatma Gandhi was more a votary of villages than towns. He believed that the soul of India lives in villages and hence his vision of Gram Swaraj and cottage industries to induce self reliance in rural India. With the commencement of NEP, the pace of urbanization has picked up in the last 20-25 years and the situation as of now is that 1 out of every 3 Indians live in villages. By the end of 2030, it is expected that around 600 million Indians would live in towns and cities. Urbanization has been made possible by rapid industrialization and increased connectivity between the rural and the urban centres. Even the rural parts of the country are undergoing attitudinal changes thanks to increased penetration of cable technology and ICT (Information Communication Technologies). Compared to rural India, caste restrictions are less in urban India though instances of blatant caste discrimination do surface from time to time.

Globalization is a broad term that should not be analyzed only in terms of investment and technology flows from one part of the globe to another, thanks to internet/ICT technology but also in the social sphere. Human resources (though highly skilled) move from one country to another to take up assignments as many of the corporate giants have multinational presence. This constant intermingling and movement from one end of the world to another results in shared understanding/purpose which hastens the process towards commonality of interests. Our society is slowly moving towards the realization of the concept of a truly global village. The food habits, the clothes we wear and the social value systems are becoming more and more homogenous. Economic turmoil in any part of the world quickly starts affecting the economies in other parts of the world as we are now witnessing how the economic turmoil in Europe/ USA are having a contagion effect on the economies of India/China/Japan. Now let us take a look at the environmental issues like emission of green house gases, global warming and ozone layer depletion. There is a growing realization of the fact that these environmental problems cannot be solved by a single nation as environmental problems of pollution/degradation have no national boundaries. Hence the coming into existence of pacts likes the Kyoto Protocol and the Montreal Protocol. The international organizations like the European Union, IMF, World Bank and UNO have gained currency in recent years and the trend is towards the unification of interests, concerns and actions. In the realm of international political relations, the groupings like ASEAN, BRICS, SAARC, G—8, G—20 etc. are nothing but the manifestation of the concerted actions of a comity of nations in unison for the fulfillment of their objectives. At a time, when the homogenization effects of globalization are more visible than ever before, it remains to be seen how a subaltern movement, speaking exclusively for dalits, survives. The identity markers are fast disappearing into an inclusive and secular dimension. It's high time the dalit movement starts thinking on the lines of global citizens and learns to identify itself with the plight of all the oppressed people of the world.

Economic reforms are here to stay in India and it is not possible to reverse the clock back. The dalit movement has to accept this reality and rather than holding back with a cynical view, it must start interrogation with the unleashed forces of globalization. NEP is not a brahminical device to tide over the loss of public employment opportunities in the aftermath of the implementation of the Mandal Commission Report and the dalit presence in public employment but it got going to offset the economic crisis into which the nation had plunged into at the start of the early nineties. India had been witness to the spectacular strides made by China and the East Asian countries in developing their economies though their development trajectory was not very different from India at the start of 1950s. All this was made possible by opting for a more open economy which gave the Asian tigers ample resources to improve the quality of life of their citizens by investment in critical sectors like health and education. The dalit leadership does not have an economic insight to appreciate the transformation taking place around the globe in economy and hence, it has not been able to adopt a consistent line on the dilemma confronting the majority of dalits as to how the neo reforms can be made congruous with dalit interests. It is very much alive to the plight of dalits most of who are suffering from acute deprivation levels. The dalit movement must advocate for making the NEP more humane and people friendly as it is here where the dalit stakes lie. It is a fact that today, the dalit groups have metamorphosed into powerful pressure lobbies and no ruling party can turn a deaf ear to their demands. The movement must use its position to enable such public policy formulation that is responsive to the needs/aspirations of the vulnerable groups. These groups must be provided with public social assistance and social security apparatus must be designed for them to protect them from the liberalization onslaught. The social security can be in the form of pensions, scholarships for students, healthcare, insurance cover in the event of accidental death of the sole bread earner of the family etc. According to the estimates of International Labour Organization, only 20 percent of the vulnerable sections of the world population have access to social security assistance and the rest are left out to fend for them. ILO points out that the social security measures have indirect benefits for the health of the economy. These schemes help in increasing the purchasing power of the weaker sections and help in generating demand in the economy.

Rather than playing the victim card, the dalit leadership/intelligentsia should take LPG as a challenge and make common cause with the non dalits in striving for imparting of a more humane face to the reform process because not only dalits but millions of non dalits at the lower and middle class levels are feeling disenchanted with the neo reform process. More than 20 years of reforms have not yielded any tangible material benefits to them. Despite high rates of GDP growth at 8 or above 8 percent in recent years, at the human development index score of 0.612, India languishes at the 134th position in the international comity of nations. Perpetual harping on caste and giving the impression that dalits have their own interests than concerns, unrelated to the rest of the population, might lead to the weakening of the more broad based secular movement advocating for pro people reform.

Ambedkar may have talked about the caste prejudices against the lower castes and denial of basic human rights to them; he may have at times appeared sectarian, solely obsessed with the dalit cause but the nation can't forget that it was the same Ambedkar who founded the Independent Indian Labour Party to articulate forcefully the concerns of the working class. He talked of the state sponsored industrialization policy, payment of remunerative wages to the labourers, just and humane conditions of work for them like fixing minimum working hours and wage payment on leave. It was the same Ambedkar who fought for the workers' right to strike in support of their genuine grievances as was demonstrated in the strife between the workers and the management in the Mumbai Textiles Mills. As the labour minister in the government of India in the early forties, he orchestrated the passing of the Minimum Wages Act. His concerns appear largely relevant today when we see the happenings, recently at a Maruti Plant in Manesar, Haryana. The workers' protest against the management took a violent turn, resulting in the death of one of the senior executives of the company. In this age of neo capitalism, the concept of state minimalism has become a vehicle for the furtherance of interests of the industry and that too, in collusion with the state machinery. The pro industry tilt of the state has adversely affected the overall industrial relations scenario in the country. The rights of the workers to form their own trade unions have been curtailed and often, the workers have no job security. Since the onset of economic reforms, industry and economy have made huge profits but the gains of growth have not been allowed to pass on to the work force whose real wages have witnessed a decline when we take inflation into account. A majority of the workers work on a contractual basis and earn something in the range of Rs. 5000-8000, half of which goes into the rent payment of their accommodations. On the other hand, capitalists are getting cheap land from the state, the natural resources are being thrown open at them at throwaway prices, tax holidays are announced for them and fiscal incentives are provided by them. All these steps are justified for accelerating the growth of the economy and attracting investment from outside. The dalit movement has simply failed to carry forward the pro working class agenda of Ambedkar and adopts an ostrich like approach when confronted with such issues. Whenever given a chance to be at the helm of affairs, the dalit leadership is not shy of going hands-in-glove with the capitalists and sharing in the loot of scarce natural resources. It is doubtful whether Ambedkar would have been just a mute spectator to this blatant exploitation of the working class labour and the common masses. He would certainly have taken up the cudgels on the behalf of the oppressed working class, a major chunk of which belongs to the weaker sections of the society.

Hardly bothered by the unfolding events, some dalit intellectuals are advocating for dalit capitalism. They are arguing that it's time for the dalits to shed their historical baggage of being seen as one surviving on state dole outs/largess and take control over their environment. They should embrace capitalism, economic reforms and globalization. For them, capitalism challenges caste and has the potential to act as a crusader against caste. Dalit capitalism is supposed to act as an instrument of dalit emancipation by facilitating them to become entrepreneurs/employers who would give employment to others rather than be seen to be depending on others for employment. It is aimed at breaking the age old historical social barriers and then restoring the self respect and pride of the dalits. The concept seemed to be inspired by the so called success of black or Afro American capitalism in USA. When we look at USA today, the society seems to be divided and unequal as never before. President Obama appears to be having a tough time in convincing the Republicans of the need of having an adequate state support for the needy and the commoners. The Afro American community provides the maximum support base to Obama today and it is they who today are facing the ugly side of global capitalism. The blacks have not gained anything substantial despite years of capitalism, and that too, in the temple of world capitalism, compelling them to remain lying at the bottom of the socio economic development pyramid in USA. Since majority of the black population lives in ghettos and slums under very trying conditions, incidences like drug addiction, petty thefts, molestations and other forms of social crimes surface. The percentage of incarcerated blacks is much more than the whites in USA. In 2011, the poverty rate among the blacks was around 30 percent while among the non Hispanic whites it was less than 10 percent. The 2008 economic crisis and the subsequent bailing out of the big private banks by the USA Govt. with the money of the tax payers led to drastic cuts in the welfare budget affecting the blacks much more than the whites. The Pew Research Centre analysis shows that that the median wealth of white households was a staggering 20 times that of black households in 2009. This was the largest gap in 25 years and almost twice the ratio before the crisis. Why USA? Even in the developed capitalist west European countries, the white population is much more economically developed than the Asian or the African communities settled there, most of who are willing to do jobs which the whites don't want to accept.

Amidst the excitement of dalits becoming capitalists and co partners in democratic capitalism, several critical points are missed. Indian capitalism is not caste immune and most of the private sector is family controlled. Several dalit entrepreneurs will amply testify for the kind of hardships they face while conducting their business operations in capitalist India. In their missionary zeal to use capitalism to cleanse the evils of our social set up, these advocates of dalit capitalism fail to see the plight and exploitation of the commoners engendered by the evils of global capitalism. The fact that they are seeking to find an equal space for dalits in this system that is exploitative, unethical and unequal is shocking. The very ideology espoused by

Ambedkar is going to be inverted or turned upside down. It is interesting to note that the dalit remedy of ending discrimination seems to be lying in capitalism, whose very advent in India in the early 1990s is blamed for leading to loss of job openings for dalits and the backwards in public employment. Capitalism, say liberalization in other words, has been castigated for lessening the scope and breadth of social justice plank in political India. The ugly side of capitalism is rearing its head and most of the welfare democratic states have been forced to abdicate several schemes for the poor. The capitalist revolution that spearheaded the industrial revolution post World War II, riding on the back of factories and a strong manufacturing base seems to have taken the back seat, with more emphasis on speculation, referred to as casino capitalism.

In the words of David Harvey—neo capitalism accumulates through dispossession—privatization of public property, forcible eviction of peasants and indigenous populations from their lands, unbridled exploitation of natural resources and so on. Rather than adopting a critical approach towards predatory capitalism, dalit capitalism tries to align itself with it. Even the great Ambedkar would have been flabbergasted to see his followers seeking the liberation of his people through capitalism.

Dalit Movement: An introduction to its growth trajectory in Indian Context

References:

1. Outcaste: Dalit movement: From where to where?
2. 1948 sequel to who were the Shudras? The untouchables: 'A thesis on the origin of untouchability'
3. B.R Ambedkar: From Wikipedia, the free encyclopedia
4. Crisis of Ambedkarites and future challenges (Anand Teltumde)
5. Dalit Panthers: Wikipedia, the free encyclopedia
6. BSP: Wikipedia, the free encyclopedia

Dalit Movement: Politics of sectarianism/ negativity/identity/exclusion

References:

1. Dalit movement at crossroads by VB Rawat, dated 9/8/05 (Countercurrents.org)
2. Ambedkar and Kanshiram: so alike and so different (Hindu dated 11/5/12)
3. On the margins of margin (Hindu dated 20/6/12)
4. Crisis of Ambedkarites and future challenges by Anand Teltumde dated 22/4/11

Impact of middle class uprising on dalit movement

References:

1. Times of India Blog—Reserving Past by Santosh Desai—dated 25/12/11

Mandalisation of polity and dalit movement

References:

1. Subhramanium (1999): Comprehensive study of Tamil Polity.

Dalit movement—Hindutva and Buddhism

References:

1. Hindutva: from Wikipedia, the free encyclopedia
2. Half a dalit revolution,
3. The political and social in dalit movement today by Harsh S. Wankhede (EPW dated 9.2.08)
4. Hindu nationalism: From Wikipedia
5. Onslaught of fascist Hindutva on dalits: Impact and Resistance (Anand Teltumde)

Reservation: the never ending syndrome

References:

1. Rethinking social justice by Yogendra Yadav

Dalit movement and the issue of land

References:

1. Nuts and bolts of appropriating agricultural land—Bhaskar Goswami
2. Nailing the lie of land by Medha Patekar (HINDU dated 23/8/12)

Dalit Movement: A victim of symbolism & patronage politics

References:

1. Dalit symbolism and the democratization of secular spaces (Harsh S. Wankhede), Mainstream dated 13/3/10.

New Economic Reforms and dalit movement

References:

1. The Chimera of dalit capitalism (Hindu) dated 19/07/2013.